T0130621

Home: A Very Short Introduction

VERY SHORT INTRODUCTIONS are for anyone wanting a stimulating and accessible way into a new subject. They are written by experts, and have been translated into more than 40 different languages.

The series began in 1995, and now covers a wide variety of topics in every discipline. The VSI library now contains over 450 volumes—a Very Short Introduction to everything from Psychology and Philosophy of Science to American History and Relativity—and continues to grow in every subject area.

Very Short Introductions available now:

Available soon:

For more information visit our website

www.oup.com/vsi/

Michael Allen Fox

HOME

A Very Short Introduction

OXFORD
UNIVERSITY PRESS

OXFORD

UNIVERSITY PRESS

Great Clarendon Street, Oxford, OX2 6DP,
United Kingdom

Oxford University Press is a department of the University of Oxford.
It furthers the University's objective of excellence in research, scholarship,
and education by publishing worldwide. Oxford is a registered trade mark of
Oxford University Press in the UK and in certain other countries

© Michael Allen Fox 2016

The moral rights of the author have been asserted

First edition published in 2016

All rights reserved. No part of this publication may be reproduced, stored in
a retrieval system, or transmitted, in any form or by any means, without the
prior permission in writing of Oxford University Press, or as expressly permitted
by law, by licence or under terms agreed with the appropriate reprographics
rights organization. Enquiries concerning reproduction outside the scope of the
above should be sent to the Rights Department, Oxford University Press, at the
address above

You must not circulate this work in any other form
and you must impose this same condition on any acquirer

Published in the United States of America by Oxford University Press
198 Madison Avenue, New York, NY 10016, United States of America

British Library Cataloguing in Publication Data

Data available

Library of Congress Control Number: 2016946826

ISBN 978-0-19-874723-9

Printed and bound by
CPI Group (UK) Ltd, Croydon, CR0 4YY

Links to third party websites are provided by Oxford in good faith and
for information only. Oxford disclaims any responsibility for the materials
contained in any third party website referenced in this work.

For my sister Robin Fox (1935–2016), who is greatly missed by three generations, and whose home was always so welcoming

And though home is a name, a word, it is a strong one; stronger than magician ever spoke, or spirit answered to, in strongest conjuration.

—Charles Dickens, *Martin Chuzzlewit* (1843–4), chap. 35

Contents

Acknowledgements

My late sister Robin Fox, my good friend Robert Banks, and my wife Louise Noble generously devoted their time to reading my entire manuscript. They also brought many useful resources to my attention. Their overall assessments, attention to detail, and acute insights have helped me produce a much better work. I am very grateful for their input.

By my count, this book has been refereed or reviewed in one way or another by Oxford University Press at least ten times prior to publication. I have learned much from all of those involved in this process, most of whose names I will never know. I wish to extend special appreciation, however, to Senior Commissioning Editor Andrea Keegan and Assistant Commissioning Editor Jenny Nugee for all their advice and encouragement, and to Joy Mellor, my wonderful Copyeditor. Deborah Protheroe, Senior Picture Researcher, has been fast and efficient in securing sources and permissions for the book's illustrations. I am also greatly indebted to my outstanding Project Manager Saraswathi Ethiraju.

The School of Humanities at the University of New England, Armidale, New South Wales, Australia, was my research base during the entire period of preparing this publication. I thank UNE for supporting my scholarly activities.

An earlier version of Chapter 1 was published in *PAN: Philosophy Activism Nature* 12 (Summer 2016).

List of illustrations

Chapter 1
The many faces of home

Thinking about home

Homes have always been gathering places. Prehistoric peoples sheltered together as best they could, and sometimes even in good style. Many, many generations later, in recorded history, the rich and famous boasted opulent salons and courts for entertaining, which were celebrated, and to which invitations were keenly sought. But humble country folk and urbanites too, in various ethnic traditions, have placed friendly hospitality at or near the top of their list of social obligations that require careful tending, and thus a warm welcome and comforting hearth could be expected in their abodes as well. These traditions continue today. Home is central to human life. Accordingly, home has been much thought about, treasured, and longed for, and abundant written works and other cultural products have been devoted to the subject. We may suppose, then, that home is a settled concept, that is, one which is transparent and readily understood. But we need to think again. Home *is* a fundamental and universal concept, yet it has multiple associated and layered meanings for different people in a great range of circumstances. It inspires deep emotions and creative expressions that are both heartfelt and more intellectual. As a result, home surprises us by turning out to be a restless, shifting, somewhat elusive notion.

When popular media focus on the home, usually our interest is directed to architecture, design, style, interior decorating, or consumer goods of a certain sort. Here, however, we will try to get clear about what home is (and might be), and how people (including ourselves) think and feel about their living spaces in relation to the world around them.

Appearance vs. reality

The word 'façade', which refers to the front of any building, has its origin in French, Italian, and Latin words for 'face', and has the secondary meaning of 'false front' or 'deceptive outward appearance'. Architect Edwin Heathcote suggests that a house may be 'a space for showing off, for presenting a face to the world'. When we view houses as homes, many of the things that go on within these dwellings are called up for investigation. So, in addition, are the varied, profound, and nuanced, often hidden thoughts and feelings that collect under the topic of home. These are 'the many faces of home'. And just as a book should not be judged by its cover, what home means only reveals itself when we look carefully beneath the surface.

Defining 'home'

'Home, sweet home' (see Figure 1)... 'Be it ever so humble, there's no place like home'... 'Home is where the heart is'... 'Home is where you come from and can be yourself'... 'The longest road out is the shortest way home'... 'Been on the road too long. It's time to get home'... 'Welcome home!'

What do we mean by 'home'? The meaning of this important word, like that of others freely used in everyday life, tends to be taken for granted. Home is just the place one takes for granted, *my* place, the place where *I* belong, feel comfortable, and can be somebody, be wanted. It contains the objects with the most personal significance and is the primary theatre within which one

1. An early cover for the sheet music of 'Home Sweet Home'.

acts out and forges an identity. Home represents solace, peace and quiet, warmth, love, acceptance—it's 'a place to hang your hat'. Thoughts of home open onto vistas of pride and remembrance—of family, country, homeland, childhood, heritage, lineage, and loyalties of various sorts (such as patriotism). Odysseus (or Ulysses), the mythical adventure hero of Homer's *Odyssey*, embodies this spirit when he yearns for his distant home in the Greek city of Ithaca, after vanquishing the Cyclops. We may be neither sung nor unsung heroes; we may not be heroes at all. But we do not find it difficult to identify with his embrace of home as dwelling and country, even many centuries later.

Odysseus, however, notwithstanding his restless voyaging, lived in a time when most people were less mobile—a time when the world was less rapidly changing than today, when home was a more certain and less contested notion. Yet he helps us understand why home is often longed for as a place of wholeness and respite from the stresses of life. As author Maya Angelou proposes, 'The ache for home lives in all of us, the safe place where we can go as we are and not be questioned.' And as philosopher Gaston Bachelard romanticizes, our childhood home fitted us like a glove, is still inscribed in our bodily memory, and remains the template for inhabiting all houses we encounter thereafter. For these writers, home is the benevolent, smiling face within the crowd of chaotic frowns that characterize the places of everyday existence. In a topsy-turvy, unsettling world, having a bolt-hole to retire to can be a blessing.

But what makes something or some place count as home? A very neutral, minimalist definition of 'home' is that it is 'any place of residence or refuge'. An amplified definition, which is closer to common usage, identifies home as 'a house, apartment, or other shelter that is the usual residence of a person, family, or household'. So far, so good. But if we could summarize home so briefly, there would be no need to examine the concept with the expectation of greater gain. And even an expanded dictionary definition ranges much further afield (Box 1). How, then, shall we begin the daunting task of explaining 'home' in all of its richness of meaning?

For most people in the world, home now designates a specific construction within a built environment—a lean-to, shed, house,

Box 1 The many origins of the word 'home'

The *Oxford English Dictionary* (*OED*) is the definitive guide to the definitions and origins (etymologies) of English words. For the word 'home', the *OED* lists cognates (words sharing a common origin) in Gothic, Old Danish, Old Dutch, Old Frisian, Old High German, Old Icelandic, Old Saxon, and Old Swedish, and suggests that this list might possibly be expanded by the addition of numerous other early European languages. The principal meanings of home found in the *OED* and their origins are as follows:

'The place where a person or animal dwells' (Origin: Old English).

'A dwelling place; a person's house or abode; the fixed residence of a family or household; the seat of domestic life and interests. Also (chiefly in later usage): a private house or residence considered merely as a building' (Origin: Old English).

'The place where one lives or was brought up, with reference to the feelings of belonging, comfort, etc. associated with it' (First usage: 1546).

'A refuge, a sanctuary; a place or region to which one naturally belongs or where one feels at ease' (Origin: Old English).

'A person's own country or native land. Also: the country of one's ancestors' (Origin: Old English).

'A place where something originates, flourishes, or is most typically found; the seat, centre, or birthplace of an activity' (First usage [disputed]: *c.*1200; well-established: 1603).

('home, n. 1 and adj.', OED Online, <www.oed.com>)

hut, mansion, apartment, or some other at least semi-permanent dwelling unit. And yet, there are still individuals and cultures for which home means something quite different. These visions include: wide-open spaces under the stars (Home on the Range; Big Sky Country); an ideal community (New Jerusalem; Utopia); a particular land (place of origin; ancestral domain); wherever the highway leads (the open road; home from home); where the gods or revered spirits traditionally reside (Valhalla; Paradise); or simply Mother Earth herself. Views of this sort spring from many sources. From the standpoint of today's mainstream cultures, some of these represent unconventional or minority perspectives, but from within the perspectives themselves, they express how the world is, and how one should relate to it.

There are thus people whose identities are intimately intertwined with home as a fixed reference point; others who believe themselves quite free of the bonds of home; those for whom home is a traditional and sacred place; and those who encounter home anywhere, everywhere, or nowhere.

Given such diversity, we may be inclined to conclude that home is merely something in the mind of the beholder. Even focusing on the narrower concept of the living space as a dwelling unit, geographers Alison Blunt and Robyn Dowling compel us to look more closely when they state that a home may be 'a tent, caravan, house, apartment, park bench, or any other assemblage of building materials on a particular site'.

As if to reinforce their point, historian Peter Watson informs us that at choreographer Rudolf Laban's celebrated pre-First World War experimental dance school in Ascona, Switzerland, 'One of the dancers lived in a harmonium crate'. Edmunds Bunkše, a geographer and cultural theorist, reports that in a modest apartment he occupied within 'a landscape of alienation' (the tumultuous end of the Soviet occupation of his native Latvia), 'my small worktable in the living room became my essential home'—a place of escape from the troubles of the world outside. He was no doubt speaking metaphorically; yet it is easy to understand how such a circumscribed space can become a micro-home, at least for a while—a centre of operations, as it were (in this case, Bunkše's bunker).

It appears evident from all this that any attempt to define home merely by invoking a brief formula will fail to do justice to our subject. Yet we should resist judging home as being an arbitrary idea and strive to consider whether, on the contrary, there are some essential ingredients that constitute having a home and being at home.

Understanding home in different languages

In 2014, a Nigerian touring stage production called *Finding Home* was performed widely across Africa—in Lagos, Accra, Nairobi, and Johannesburg. Using a mixture of spoken poetry and theatre, this show focused on the personal complexities of migration abroad and reverse migration to the place of origin. *Finding Home* demonstrated people's ability to comprehend the meaning of home at a deeper (or more basic) level in spite of cultural and linguistic differences.

At the same time, however, it would be a mistake to simply equate the terms used for home by diverse language groups. English speakers can call upon a distinct and well-developed apprehension of home that is embedded in their language. The English word 'home' has clearly documented early linguistic origins, as we've seen, but these may demonstrate its somewhat unique character as much as its age.

Linguistics scholar Anna Wierzbicka cautions against assuming that English provides an adequate standard for evaluating the meanings of words in other languages. Doing so not only leads to verbal misunderstandings (where subtleties of meaning are overlooked), but also displays a cultural arrogance that prevents us from communicating with speakers of different languages on equal terms. Still, Wierzbicka does believe that, notwithstanding the great abundance of languages across the globe, there is 'a core of simple words and concepts where all languages meet'. Indeed, it is difficult to see how it could be otherwise, if learning other languages and translating them is to be at all possible.

Two things become clear from this discussion—first, that what is meant by 'home' in English may lack an exact counterpart in other languages; and, second, that words in different languages used to describe a dwelling will pick out different aspects of experience and significance that contrasting cultures regard as vital.

In English, 'home' stands for a place of residence, belonging, and attachment—more broadly, it bestows familiarity, attraction, warmth of feeling, pride, a special sense of bonding, and other important characteristics onto dwellings, geographical locations, nations, and traditional regions in which spiritual, ethnic, religious, and historical identities are formed and dovetail into a sense of self.

In this wider context, self and home are inseparable elements, with each depending on the other for its existence and properties (see Chapter 6). This vision of home is tapped into when people say things like: 'I am Russian', or 'I have my roots in that place', or 'My ancestors and the spirits that made this land dwell here'. Architect Witold Rybczynski observes that

> This wonderful word 'home', which connotes a physical 'place' but also has the more abstract sense of a 'state of being', has no equivalent in the Latin or Slavic European languages. German, Danish, Swedish, Icelandic, Dutch, and English all have similar sounding words for 'home', all derived from the Old Norse 'heima'.

Anthropologist Jerry Moore, meanwhile, traces a connection between an early Germanic linguistic form, via Lithuanian, to a Sanskrit word *ksêmas* ('safe or secure dwelling, abode, or refuge'), which suggests that the origins of the English word 'home' may be quite diverse. While one can perhaps accept that similar sounding words sharing a common origin also possess a closely related semantic scope, it is more difficult to know how to reconcile words that are very dissimilar. Consider the following examples:

In Yankunytjatjara, an Aboriginal dialect of the Western Desert region of Australia, there is the word *ngura*, which translates more closely to 'place', 'camp', or 'country' than to 'home'.

The Polish word *dom*, even though it has Greek and Latin roots, refers to a dwelling unit ('house' or 'home') but also embraces group values relating to homeland.

The Hebrew word *bayit* means both 'home' and 'house', and also references the place where Jewish family life is grounded.

The Nootka First Nations people of Canada's Vancouver Island traditionally lived in immense 'plankhouse' structures, in which several families had assigned spaces and carried out their daily activities. These could be disassembled and moved to a new location as needed. For this reason, as one anthropologist states, 'house' is more of a verb than a noun: 'In Nootka, you don't say "house", but "it houses", or "a house occurs" because for the Nootka, houses are impermanent'. Transportability is built into the word itself, which explains the awkwardness of its English translation.

Each of these examples extends the meaning of words that describe dwelling places beyond the simple property-based formula of 'house + identifiable parcel of land' that prevails in cultures dominated by commerce, capitalism, and the real estate industry.

There is no need, then, to put forward a prescriptive (or stipulative) definition of 'home' that is intended to cover all languages. But it might help if we adopt the philosopher Ludwig Wittgenstein's notion of 'family resemblance'. Wittgenstein claimed that for many words—his favourite example was 'game', but he also included the word 'language' itself—there is no essential set of features that everything those words single out must possess. Whatever such a word refers to or describes need only satisfy some range of characteristics within a larger totality in order to be used correctly in a given context. This approach seems to be strengthened by the linguists' quest for common concepts that enable cross-cultural understanding. Following this strategy, we can now simply say that the ideas of home located in various languages share (or partake of) a pool of common properties which they draw upon in different ways.

Attitudes towards home

Many people's experience of home is entirely or largely positive, as witness the pieces of folk wisdom quoted earlier. This includes those who have had the benefit of a domestic environment that is safe, supportive, loving, and encourages the individual to flourish. Some seem to just *know* that the place they grow up in—both the dwelling and its location—is where they are 'meant to be', at least for that period of time. And they may always carry this sense of home with them so that it remains a place they can comfortably visit.

Yet homecoming, after a prolonged period of absence, is often an experience fraught with emotional baggage that is difficult to face and deal with (see Chapter 4). Hence, for some it will be a mixed blessing, and for others a confounding, destabilizing, even alienating or toxic scenario. Everything's the same, but everything's changed. One doesn't 'fit' here anymore—or maybe one realizes one never did.

And what of people whose negative associations with home make it the place they urgently need to escape from and avoid ever after?

Alongside those who have been harmed there, this group includes some who just find the home environment boring and stifling. William Shakespeare wrote, "'Tis ever common/That men are merriest when they are from home'. Samuel Taylor Coleridge amplified as follows: 'The largest part of mankind are nowhere greater strangers than at home'. And 20th-century American playwright Thornton Wilder has one of his theatrical characters humorously reflect that 'Everybody's always talking about people breaking into houses...; but there are more people in the world who want to break out of houses'. Home, like a magnet, can both attract and repel. The group identified by Wilder's character has been labelled 'domophobic' (home-fearful or home-averse) by Clare Cooper Marcus, an expert on the psychology of home, because it includes individuals who have experienced serious forms of abuse and oppression at home.

For still others, having a home may be an unlived, phantom condition, or only a distant memory, a half-lived, or now-lost experience. This is the reality for those called 'homeless'—a very large and disturbingly increasing category of people worldwide (see Chapter 7).

So we do need to recognize that, despite the sentimental adages with which we clothe it, home does not always strike a positive chord with everyone. It may be a warm nest for some, even for most, but not for those whose life experiences exist outside the margins of an idealized, airbrushed notion of home. Equally important, these perspectives do not represent either/or, black-or-white alternatives, because for any given individual, home may conjure up both good and bad feelings; pleasure and pain.

Parochialism and cosmopolitanism

People who have lived in the same town all their lives seem to possess something enviable, such as an identification with the

locale and the land. Perhaps they also feel a more precise
sense of their point of origin, place in society, and range of
possibilities. American storyteller Garrison Keillor, speaking
autobiographically, says a hometown contains 'the geography of a
man's life'. These attributes of place can encourage people to be
content with where they are, or to venture forth and see the world
with the recognition that they *come from somewhere significant
and definite*, a place that is always their beckoning final
destination (see Chapter 2).

However, equally possible (at least in mainstream cultures) is that
those with this sense of home possess only a *limited* view of self
and possibility, an outlook that may be far from desirable. They
may lack the wider perspective of individuals who travel a lot,
have a greater feel for adventure, or see themselves in some
fashion as 'citizens of the world'. Broadening one's experience can
lead to greater understanding and empathy, and, in effect, creates
a larger self. During a year spent in a small farming village in the
Swabian region of southern Germany, an elderly grandmother,
dressed in a traditional style, told me that 'Heimat ist immer
besser' ('One's home [or homeland or region] is always a better
place to be'). But is it? Perhaps this is true only for someone who
has a role within a customary ethnic and geographical setting that
is satisfying and meaningful to him or her, and whose expectations
and sense of purpose are relatively fixed.

In the 16th century, Michel de Montaigne, French essayist and
pioneer in charting the dynamics of self-knowledge, posited a
need to broaden one's awareness beyond the safe harbour of
the familiar:

> Human judgment gains a marvellous clarity from regular travel in
> the world. We are entirely constrained and wrapped up in ourselves,
> and our short-sighted outlook only reaches the end of our
> nose.... This great world... is the mirror in which we must see
> ourselves in order to know ourselves properly.... Such an

abundance of temperaments, sects, judgments, opinions, laws, and customs teaches us to judge carefully ourselves and conditions our judgment to recognize its own imperfection and natural weakness: this is no insignificant lesson.

Keenly observing the world is essential to life-education. But notice that Montaigne does not say travelling and interacting with the strange and unfamiliar merely *enhances* our view of the world, but rather that it makes us engage in self-examination and questioning of accepted norms that prevail 'back home'. Montaigne champions *liberation of the mind* from the stultifying influences of what we are accustomed to, which contrasts with a quietly accepting and complacently affirmative attitude towards home.

Even though living in multicultural societies and using the Internet tend to undercut the distinction between 'home' and 'away', there is still much to be gained from venturing forth from home. Dan Kieran, a contemporary writer, makes the novel suggestion that we travel in order to recover ways of knowing about the world that have been eradicated by our own culture, but remain preserved and practised elsewhere. This fascinating thought truly runs through the wringer some of the more traditional ideas about home.

As an aside, however, we may note that it takes a certain kind of person to seek a broader vision of things in the first place, for as another proverb teaches, 'If an ass goes travelling it will not come home a horse'.

Home as a restless concept

The philosopher G.W.F. Hegel argues that we always progress in our lives to more advanced levels of meaning that transform, but at the same time incorporate, the elements we think we've left behind. Becoming a citizen of the world, then, does not enable us to leave home behind entirely, even if this is our wish, because home always travels with us, preserved in some form or other, and we cannot shake it off any more than an atheist can completely shake off God when developing an alternative approach to life, or a snail or clam can shed its shell. The outcome, it would appear, is that the need to know what home means is inescapable for those who want to live their lives with greater intelligence and awareness—whether they also wish to embrace or reject what being at home has meant to them until now.

We come to the conclusion, then, that home, for all of its immediate and more traditional associations, is actually a multi-faceted, problematic notion, and for many, an almost undefinable thing, a *je ne sais quoi* ('I know not what'). Home is somewhere definite; anywhere; I'm-not-sure-where; somewhere-yet-to-be; or an imaginary and distant somewhere. It may be comforting and reassuring; or scary and repellent (or both). It may be a firm or a fragile, unstable presence. It may beckon from nearby or vanish over the horizon. This makes it an alluring phenomenon to investigate—for in one guise or another it plays a key role in our lives.

Chapter 2
The importance of place

Place and the organization of life

Whatever else it might be, home is a place. This may be a spatial place or a place in the memory or imagination, or a place in all these senses plus more besides—such as an environment that is endowed with spiritual or symbolic significance. A 'home place' is also actively fashioned by those who inhabit it or are believed to, including human subjects and vitalizing forces (for example, ancestral or legendary presences). We must, therefore, when thinking about home, be prepared to stretch our concept of place in order to accommodate quite different dimensions of meaning.

Everyone has an ordinary sense of place—of being located or established somewhere at a given time; but when a place is noteworthy we also have a sense of *what it means for us to be there*. Novelist, poet, and essayist David Malouf observes that 'one of the ways—a necessary one—by which we come at last into full possession of a place…[is] in the imagination', and this is where the work of writers, painters, photographers, and our own creative powers takes over. Some places attract us and are comfortable to be in, others fall short. Some are chosen by us, others are not, such as places of birth, confinement, or exile. The notion of place is in part a cultural construct, as when the coordinates of a given location are described by compass points, longitude and latitude, or what occurred there in mythological time. Places are where 'we live and move and have our being', to borrow a biblical expression. When a place is apprehended as special or extraordinary, our orientation towards it amounts to something very concrete: we experience the impact on us of its positive or negative energy. As artist and conservationist Alan Gussow puts it simply, 'A place is a piece of the whole environment that has been claimed by feelings.' And this is the level at which the iconic representations contributed by the imagination help us to settle ourselves in the world.

Attitudes towards place may be more or less perceptive and sophisticated, and either well or poorly articulated. Even within the same cultural tradition, people differ widely in the ability to appreciate their surroundings: Some have little or no interest in them; others are neutral towards them; still others value and affirm their importance to varying degrees; a few are passionately committed to a spot they cherish as completely exceptional. 'Is this where we live, I thought, in this place at this moment, with the air so light and wild?' writes Annie Dillard in *Pilgrim at Tinker Creek*. What do we identify with when we call a place our own? A given environment? A cultural, language or religious affiliation? A kinship lineage? Family and friends? A neighbourhood? Some combination of these? When we think of home, where is it? And where is everything else in relation to home?

The home place

People often have a larger engagement with home than they realize or acknowledge. To start with, home is a location, small or large, that serves as a base from which activities in the world are planned and undertaken. Home may be somewhere we return to merely out of habit; because we love it and feel we belong there; need a special place to rejuvenate ourselves for the next round of worldly pursuits; just want a roof over our heads and a bed to sleep in; or for many other reasons. We may be utterly pragmatic in our choice of abode, or fanciful and desirous (Box 2).

Box 2 Homes come in an incredible range of sizes

The production of very compact, environmentally sensible homes is a thriving business. Called 'tiny houses' (often less than 400 square feet, or 37.16 square metres), these dwellings are fashioned out of every material or object from weatherboard to boats to shipping containers and old railroad cars. Meanwhile, 'micro-apartments'—some as small as 161.5 square feet (15 square metres)—are being built in New York and Melbourne.

Increasing affluence promotes the construction of large houses and other dwelling units in countries as far separated as Australia, the United States, China, Denmark, and Azerbaijan—even when family size remains stable or actually decreases. But today's typical large homes are no match for the gargantuan, ostentatious, oversized structures of the past and present. The beautiful 18th-century English country house in Yorkshire known as Wentworth Woodhouse has 365 rooms and 5 miles (8 km) of corridors. This home is dwarfed, in turn, by Antilla, a controversial twenty-seven-storey custom-built skyscraper colossus built in Mumbai for billionaire Mukesh Ambani and his family. It is reputed to be the largest and most expensive home ever built at 400,000 square feet (37,161 square metres). It contains every amenity imaginable, including six floors of parking space, a two-storey health centre, floating gardens, and a Hindu temple. But Antilla itself is easily eclipsed by the Sultan of Brunei's Istana Nurul Iman palace, with its staggering size of 2,152,782 square feet (200,000 square metres), that encompasses 1,788 bedrooms, 257 bathrooms, 564 chandeliers, 44 staircases, and 18 elevators.

(Ryan Mitchell, *Tiny Houses*)

Home embodies specific meanings for each of us, which are influenced by various push and pull factors. Disabled individuals may experience their homes as a positive challenge and/or a source of frustration. But personal attitude and degree of determination are crucial to how they perceive and negotiate home. This underscores the observation made by Julie Beck, an editor at *The Atlantic* magazine, that 'home isn't just where you are, it's who you are'.

Whatever the size or type of a home, it is always *situated* in important respects. And this is true in relation to both its natural and humanly created environs and geopolitical position. Otto Bollnow, a German philosopher specializing in phenomenology (the detailed description of different types of experience), singles out home as the point of reference from which we define our outlook on the world:

[H]owever we look at it, in some sense we can certainly say that [a person] is home somewhere. And that [a] *house* is the reference point from which [one] builds [one's] spatial world.

But it would certainly be exaggerated and wide of the mark to call the individual house the center of a [person's] space. As the individual does not live alone but has a certain position as a member in a community, so also [one's] house stands in a membered spatial surrounding.... [E]ven today, if I live on the edge of a city I look to some perhaps not too localizable central point in 'the city'. Difficult as it may be to find it in a particular instance, there is such a middle point of life-filled space which is no longer the space of the individual..., but of the group and ultimately of the nation to which [she or he] belongs.

Bollnow is getting at the idea that the way we single out and experience our home is a function of greater organizational entities that also occupy space and that contain and contextualize the home. A particular house is a unique place because one resides there. But its placement is far from arbitrary. Furthermore, one orients oneself spatially from 'home as reference point' outwards. It is as if home constitutes a central core where we exist, lodged within a series of ever more inclusive spheres.

A dwelling is thus a place with navigational significance, but it is not and cannot be an absolute reference point or self-contained realm ('the center of a [person's] space') because it is decentred by larger frames of significance (neighbourhood, city, nation, and so on—see Figure 2). This orientation compels a home-dweller to be

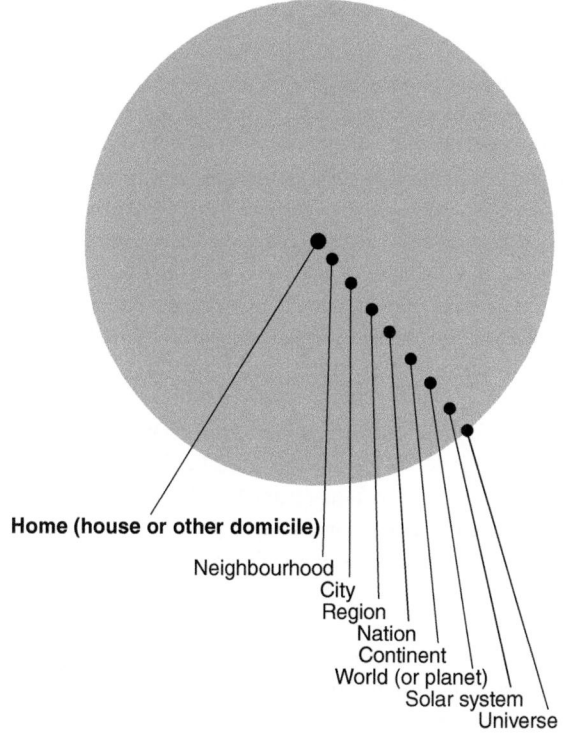

Home (house or other domicile)
Neighbourhood
City
Region
Nation
Continent
World (or planet)
Solar system
Universe

2. **Is home the centre of one's space or just an important geopolitical reference point?**

aware of what is going on in the wider world, and to take that into account in living her or his life. Thus, Bollnow suggests a kind of subterranean, unsettling conflict between one's gut feeling that home is the secure centre of things and the thoughtful realization that this is just one home among many, a place among places, depending for its very existence upon more substantial social and geographical realities, the good will of others, public services and administration, and so forth.

Geographer Edward Relph offers a 21st-century update to the kind of view Bollnow sought to develop in the mid-20th. Relph focuses on place rather than space, arguing that

> home appears through specific places yet also transcends them; it is an experience that simultaneously is rooted in a particular, familiar, meaningful place and yet opens into wonder at the differentiation of the world. From this it follows that every home, and indeed every place, is simultaneously grounded and boundless. We know from our own experience that there is no contradiction in this; I am situated here, in this room in my house or in this café on a local street, drinking fair trade coffee from El Salvador made in an Italian machine, thinking about somewhere else, or reading e-mail from friends in far-away cities.

According to Bollnow, home is somewhere that appears to function as the centre of one's existence, but overflows into, and is reflexively defined by, larger geopolitical and natural spheres. For him, home becomes a many-layered concept and reality; but the process of thinking about and describing where one lives exhibits an inner tension, as noted earlier. Relph, on the other hand, recasts this picture of home as liberating, because of the enhancements of experience brought about by knowledge, technology, the formative presence within one's own private world of elements from other cultures, and the limitless possibilities of imagination. He sees no conflict among the expansive and overlapping orientations that define home. We may or may not have visited the far-away cities where our friends reside. No matter: we can communicate with them instantly and enjoy the benefits of this wondrously enlarged human community that is available to everyone today.

Embeddedness

Martin Heidegger, another German philosopher of the 20th century, believes human life is understood by examining in depth the dimensions of everyday experience. In his essay *Building Dwelling Thinking*, Heidegger argues that we inhabit the world by dwelling in a place, and suggests that the German word *bauen* (to build) can be traced from Old High German, Old Saxon, and Gothic words meaning 'to remain, to stay in a place'. The lesson he draws from this is not the one we might expect (building enables dwelling), but precisely the opposite—that we are dwellers and therefore we build. What is it to be a dweller? Heidegger argues that dwelling is developing roots in a place such that one is at home there. His unique conception is that this involves being settled and 'at peace' in relation to the Earth, the sky, divinities, and the social fabric of which we are a part. These alignments form a unity and reveal the human setting within the matrix of Being as a whole. Heidegger tries to make it clear that humans, so situated, should naturally have, and cultivate in themselves, an attitude of caring towards the Earth and their place on it—a quite influential idea about environmental responsibility that he shares with both indigenous and non-indigenous writers.

Whether Heidegger's approach appeals to us or not, we can see where he is going with this line of reasoning. A valued place is somewhere one belongs, is part of, or dwells in; it is from this place that one's life emerges and (in the larger sense) to which it returns at death. So being *in* (and *from*) a place integrates one's life, but its significance also assumes rather cosmic proportions. Most of us will find some of Heidegger's thought congenial, since we do experience certain places as having special qualities and importance. But modern life, for many, is lived among a number of places and there may be less inclination to pronounce any of them as home once and for all, and exclusively.

More ancient views that still exist at the vital core of some societies tell a different story. Indigenous peoples, such as Australian Aborigines, members of North American First Nations, and African tribal societies, experience the places they live in as ancestral lands. Beyond the historically and scientifically verifiable fact that people genetically related to them have lived there for countless generations, this sort of vision carries with it the idea of their forebears' active spiritual presence in the land. By this it is meant that ancestral images and voices animate nature, manifest themselves as traces in, or emanating from, the landscape, and define the place. This process yields ethical, ecological, and spiritual guidance for those who live there, as well as stipulating the social rules and practices descendants in that place must adhere to. Within such a framework of belief, place is a region of intense concern—a stable axis for identity-building—that calls upon its rightful inhabitants to engage in full-time stewardship of their surroundings.

The Australian Aboriginal outlook known to the wider world as 'the Dreaming' (or 'Dreamtime') entails that the Earth is sacred (because inhabited by original and always-present creative spirits); that all living things share a unity of being; and that today's generations are custodians of the land (which is not, and can never be, a commodity). These precepts are culturally transmitted and reinforced in songs, as Aboriginal legal scholar Irene Watson explains: 'Songs are about the life of the ancestors from the Dreaming. Songs are sung of creation, our relationship to the Dreaming and our place in the land. Songs are also like a map of the country and are able to record details in the landscape.' ('Songlines' are descriptive geo-spiritual narratives that incorporate directions for using natural formations in order to navigate across great distances.) There are thus numerous ways of capturing the relationship to land that defines the sense of home for people in this tradition. Modern Aboriginal paintings on canvas, originating in the early 1970s and now part of the public record of human aesthetic/spiritual experience, opened up a stunning new medium for expressing aspects of the Dreaming, and revealed a way of thinking about place that is strikingly novel and yet timeless.

In Maori society, similar principles are at work. As anthropologist Anne Salmond reports,

> A child would often be taught a particular account [of localized ancestral history] *in that place*, so that the place and its knowledge were one, and the place and its name became a guarantee for the truth-value of the account—'I know it is true, because I have seen that very rock'. At the same time the place serves to bring the account into present time (much as documents serve us in Western histories) so that the past has existence in the present.

This is a different, but as Salmond points out not so totally foreign, approach to knowledge and evidence for truth-claims compared to the one Western cultures operate with. The Maori tradition shows once again the central importance of place to the way life should be lived, and the dependence on the land of self-identity and cultural identity.

Placelessness and beyond

The abundant influences and effects of mass culture are often seen as antagonistic to the notion of place as a meaningful location. In discussions of this issue, a contrast between place and 'placelessness' is frequently drawn. Placelessness represents standardization and monotony such as we find in the endless replication of automobile dealerships, convenience stores, petrol stations, grocery chains, shopping centres, complex layered highway interchanges, and built-to-plan suburban housing. Many have observed for themselves (and it is well-documented by social critics and historians) how automobiles have transformed everyday life, and that the outskirts of every North American city of an appreciable size are virtually identical. Paradoxically, although the places just listed are focal points of intense and familiar types of activity, they seem in a certain sense to be dead or inert or idling spaces, which raises the interesting question of whether cars control us more than we care to admit. Juxtaposed to this are the special localities and environments that do genuinely assert the uniqueness of place and offer rootedness, solace, and renewal to those who live and visit there.

But perhaps this judgement is a bit too harsh and one-sided? Might there be room for both serviceable *and* more inherently significant places to coexist side-by-side? Suburbs are growing pretty much everywhere in the world, and in some cases faster than people are reclaiming city centres. And aren't suburban developments places that many choose to live in for very good reasons, and which they often attempt to beautify and improve by efforts aimed at creating a sense of community? In this spirit, Relph proposes taking a broader perspective:

> Place and placelessness exist in a state of dynamic balance.... There are potential problems as well as advantages at either extreme. Too much place can lead to parochialism; too much placelessness results in the confusions and disappointments of a surfeit of sameness. In between there is a multitude of possibilities that reflect the character of the tension between difference and sameness.

It is important to add here that in any event, the word 'placelessness', as used thus far, is merely shorthand for something like 'site with little or no individuality or differentiating marks'. In this way of looking at things, there are just more and less interesting places to be in or to identify with. There is nothing new in that. Nonetheless, 'placeless places', for better or worse, form part of contemporary urban and non-urban human environments, and the fact that they exist tells us something important. People have different standards, and some are more capable of being at home in a given spot than others. There are those who experience shopping centres, for example, as severing connections in the community by replacing family-run businesses, covering quality land with tarmac, and increasing noise pollution and traffic congestion. But others tend to focus more on their providing improved local availability of consumer goods, employment opportunities, lower prices, and new social meeting venues.

Placeless places are not unique to modern consumerist societies. Many cultures have designated places where things (including human waste and dead bodies) are disposed of. But industrial nations throughout their history seem to have specialized in creating dismal ghettos and faceless pockets of desolation, such as no-go zones of pollution and derelict manufacturing premises. Open pit mines, oil refineries, power stations, military weapons testing grounds, neglected roadside zoos, undistinguished and indistinguishable cement-block housing projects, rubbish-strewn dockyards, empty lots containing sorrowful remnants of abandoned human activity—these places are nightmarish, unsafe, depressing landscapes of ugliness and alienation. They are not places anyone can easily identify with, even if he or she believes they somehow arise out of necessity, given a certain economic and political system. Do you want to live in or near such places? If given a choice, almost everyone would say, 'No, thank you' and 'Not in my backyard' (NIMBY). We may rebel against the idea and image of these placeless places, but we also accept that things like national security, increased standards of living, and economic growth come at a price. The question is whether and how much we are willing to sacrifice in terms of lifestyle and 'progress' in order to minimize the negative impacts of such places. Alternatively, it is a question of whether and how much we are willing to commit ourselves to seeking sustainable solutions and

more responsible long-term practices that are for the greater
benefit of all.

Landscapes, ecosystems, and bioregions

Much has been written about places as determinants of home and
home-feeling (a sense of being at home). The strongest marker of
place across cultures is no doubt the land. In recent times, many
authors have argued that it is urgent to rethink the relationship
between humans and their environment. A new perspective is
needed, they maintain—one that does not elevate the human
sphere above nature or see the two in opposition; and that
recognizes the impact of places in shaping their inhabitants' lives
and cultures.

Some have also made the case for a more harmonious sense of
place. Anthropologist Barbara Bender prompts us to consider
that what we call a *landscape* is what is 'understood, experienced,
and engaged with through human consciousness and active
involvement'. As such, it is a 'volatile' concept, which explains why
there are plentiful 'possibilities for disagreement about, and
contest over, landscape'.

One attempt to avoid this kind of conflict combines landscape and
ecosystem in the notion of a 'bioregion'. The resulting perspective,
'bioregionalism', asserts that a sense of locality is essential to who
we are. Being anchored and having a meaningful life depend upon
understanding the place where we live and our impact on it in a
more profound way than is usual, which intertwines ecology,
history, aesthetics, symbolism, and other related dimensions of
human experience. Decentralized decision-making, sustainability,
and preservation of biodiversity are also among the core ideas that
shape this outlook. Bioregions as often as not extend across
political boundaries, just as cultural and linguistic identities do.
While it is arguable that many people who live in a particular
bioregion are oblivious to its unique features, others revere and

respect its ecological integrity and inherent beauty. Cities may be included in bioregions or may be considered bioregions in themselves, so it would be a mistake to exclude them from this type of perspective—both because the experience of city living is vitally determined by geographical and environmental factors, and because detaching cities from bioregions encourages unsustainable urban development.

Cities as places

There is nonetheless a well-established tendency to drive a wedge between what is natural and what is the product of human hands and ingenuity, and this is especially notable when cities are up for discussion. Canadian ecologist and wilderness advocate Stan Rowe reflects: 'To be at home on the planet and welcome here, humanity must understand and appreciate the primacy of that home, the Eden we have never left, and the wild that is its emblem.' Perhaps most people today would agree that wilderness areas must be preserved, and to this extent the value of wilderness has become less controversial over time. Some inspired defenders of wilderness, however, have (either explicitly or by implication) excommunicated cities from ecological consideration and evaluation. Jean-Jacques Rousseau acerbically declared in the 1700s that

> Men were not made to be massed together in herds, but to be scattered over the earth which they are to cultivate. The more they herd together the more they corrupt one another....Cities are the graves of the human species....Send your children away, therefore, so that they may renew themselves, so to speak, and regain, among the fields, the vigor they have lost in the unwholesome air of places too thickly peopled.

A century later, Henry David Thoreau opined that 'Hope and the future for me are not in lawns and cultivated fields, not in towns and cities, but in the impervious and quaking swamps.' And as

John Muir more pointedly asserted, in 1901, 'going to the mountains is going home'. These important and influential thinkers obviously had no use for cities. We must remember, however, that they lived in a period (the mid-18th century to the early 20th) when even those cities that offered opportunities of various kinds and cultural jewels for the discerning were simultaneously vast industrialized machines for crushing the human spirit. Poverty, overcrowding, inadequate housing, and neglect of neighbourhoods contributed significantly to alienation, crime, violence, disease, and other social ills, and the burden of these conditions came down most heavily upon those who were mired in abominable squalor. (In spite of the importance of place, humans have—puzzlingly—done a pretty good job of fouling their own nests.) Bill Bryson informs us that in the early 19th century,

> Crowding in London districts was almost unimaginable....In Spitalfields,...inspectors found sixty-three people living in a single house. The house had nine beds—one for every seven occupants....

> [A]n inspector recorded visiting two houses in St. Giles where the cellars were filled with human waste to a depth of three feet.

> At Leeds in the 1830s, a survey of the poorer districts found that many streets were 'floating with sewage'....In Liverpool, as many as one-sixth of the populace lived in dark cellars...

These habitations nevertheless represented home for large numbers of people.

Cities then had, and continue to have, their enormous problems. But the solution is not for everyone to live in the wilderness; nor could we all realistically aspire to do so. A one-sided, romanticized, turn-back-the-clock approach that pits cities against wilderness, hinterland, or countryside is no longer relevant in the way it once may have seemed. For the demographic shift from countryside to urban centres is, quite simply, a steady and striking feature of our era. We have to deal with it. According to the World Health Organization,

> The urban population in 2014 accounted for 54% of the total global population, up from 34% in 1960, and continues to grow. Urban population growth, in absolute numbers, is concentrated in the less developed regions of the world. It is estimated that by 2017, even in less developed countries, a majority of people will be living in urban areas.

In India alone, the rate of flow from rural to urban areas amounts to ten million people annually. Water shortages in the Middle East and North Africa are also driving people to cities. These facts suggest that an enormous amount of attention is needed in order to transform cities into sustainable, safe places that people find pleasant to live in and comfortable to call 'home'.

In spite of, and even because of, the population swing just discussed, most large cities have well-defined districts or neighbourhoods, and many of these have attractive hubs, with shops, galleries, cafés, parks, community gardens, theatres, interesting laneways, waterways, street festivals, and other features and events that draw residents and visitors alike to their precincts. These provide their unique character. Cities such as Paris, London, Berlin, New York, Tokyo, Rome, Amsterdam, Copenhagen, Seoul, Chennai (formerly Madras), and São Paolo have of course possessed their respective identities for centuries, but even in these sprawling urban areas, new neighbourhoods inevitably crop up as they expand, and old neighbourhoods develop differently from what they have been in the past by virtue of immigration, gentrification, changes in the cost of housing, shifts in patterns of dining, shopping, and leisure activities, the opening of parks and new transport corridors, and so on. How people vote with their feet and money, as well as investors' and developers' preferences may be key factors in propelling these trends, rather than any systematic urban planning. Gentrification not only changes the face of neighbourhoods but also makes them unaffordable to many who've grown up there and still call them 'home'.

Smaller cities (under one million population), like Portland, Oregon (US), Nizwa (Oman), Salta (Argentina), Johannesburg (South Africa), and Bruges (Belgium), are also renowned for the singularity of their neighbourhoods. For each site, patterns in the ebb and flow of energy, land development, availability and quality of water, provision of nutrients for human and nonhuman consumption, the size of human and nonhuman populations, supplies of materials for all other purposes, the treatment of living and dead matter and wastes, the flow of traffic and people, and miscellaneous human activities are the main dynamics that determine the city's impact on its natural setting—and hence, what sort of place it is.

Place and a sense of wholeness

The momentousness of place in shaping human evolution, history, the distinctiveness of cultural groups, present-day political realities, and the character of individual lives cannot be overestimated. What we think of a place and enjoy or lament about it is determined by a great many factors, both human and non-human. These shape our sense of what and where we call 'home'. Yet the reverse is also true. Home—however it is conceived—forms an intimate aspect of our view of place. As Relph observes,

> Home in its most profound form is an attachment to a particular setting, a particular environment, in comparison with which all other associations with places have only a limited significance. It is the point of departure from which we orient ourselves and take possession of the world.

He describes here a process of becoming grounded and moving forth—not to conquer the world but to deal with its complexities and assert oneself as an effective and productive self, a self who is an agent, a distinctive being-in-the-world.

We all have a basic need for some sort of emplacement or situatedness that gives stability and satisfaction to our lives. If we are lucky enough to find it or be able to create it for ourselves, we will have reached an ideal state of affairs, which can have an important formative influence on the direction our lives take and on our conception of home. We will have found the place where we were meant to be—or at least a place where it is good to be, that feels right, and where we can settle. As the saying goes, this insight will have come home to us.

Chapter 3
Dwelling and dwellings

What dwelling means

Chapter 2 introduced the idea of humans as dwellers on the Earth. The word 'dwelling' seems to capture as well as any the idea of abiding in or occupying a place somewhere which is thought of as home. And it has the merit of embracing the astonishing number of structures and methods for inhabiting the world that our species has creatively devised over time. Yet it is another paradox of our topic that the word 'dwell' has itself undergone a dramatic change in meaning while evolving to its modern usage. In Old English, *dwellan* meant 'to mislead or deceive, make a fool of, lead astray'; and the Old High German *twellen* translates as 'to hinder or delay'. For reasons unknown, however, Middle English appropriated a connection with the Old Norse word *dvelja*: 'delay, tarry, stay, linger', and, by the 13th century, established 'make a home' as the meaning of 'dwell', which has carried forward to the present. It is fortunate that things turned out this way, for we very much need concepts that can help us embrace the broad range of human invention and endeavour involved in designing and producing structures that serve as house and home.

Dwelling is both an activity and a location in which that activity takes place. This is why, as anthropologist Mary Douglas points out, 'home is not only a space, it also has some structure in time'.

In Chapter 2, we also looked at the more general role of place in understanding what home means. The present chapter highlights a few of the great variety of abodes in which dwelling has occurred or does so today, and reflects further on the deep significance that may be attached to dwelling.

Throughout prehistory and history, dwellings have been conceived of and built to serve immediate practical purposes, and have therefore used readily available materials and layouts that are convenient and suitable for a specific environmental context. A natural outcome, then, would be that they expressed a certain harmony with the world around them. Later, with the intensive development of technology and industry, the emergence of architecture as a regulated profession, and the rise of moneyed classes, the design of dwellings became subject to new demands and preferences. Wealthy and powerful rulers, families, priests, warriors, and the like frequently have bigger, more lavish dwellings, but more egalitarian societies have also existed. There have also been movements, as at the present time, self-consciously directed towards living closer to the land and more sustainably—building with traditional materials and skills.

Despite this passing parade of possibilities, however, an important truth remains, as Jerry Moore observes: 'More than passive backdrops to human actions, our dwellings reflect and shape our lives.... [D]wellings are a pivotal place around which humans construct cultural meanings.' Here and in Chapter 4, we will discover how symbolic meaning has been attached to human dwellings from the distant past to the present.

Cave, sweet cave

We are accustomed to thinking of our remote human ancestors and prehistoric hominids as cave dwellers. Clearly, some were, although it is argued they were relatively few in the overall picture, chiefly because caves were not particularly pleasant places to live in, nor were they always internally stable, and wild animals often occupied them. On the plus side, caves provided very good shelter as well as being cool in summer and warm in winter. Archaeological evidence from South Africa shows that cave dwelling occurred there at least two million years ago. The remains of caves that were living spaces, fashioned to some degree by human hands, are also found in western Asia, China, Israel, and parts of Europe (for example, Matera, Italy and Guadix, Spain).

There are plentiful examples of more recent existing structures around the world that might also be described as caves. The Anasazi First Nations cliff dwellings at Mesa Verde, Colorado, US, were occupied for only a short period around 1200–1300 CE. 'The structures ranged in size from one-room storage units to villages of more than 150 rooms', says the National Park Service, and it was by very precarious approaches that they could be reached at all with supplies and water. Similarly situated dwellings have been found in Mali and in Georgia, on the Black Sea. The Guyaju hewn-rock-face complex near Beijing, of unknown origin, contains 110 stone rooms. Modifications of natural volcanic cone-shaped formations are striking presences in the Cappadocia region of Turkey (see Figure 3) and in the East Azerbaijan Province of Iran. These are well-insulated, multi-storey houses, shared by humans and their animals for many hundreds of years, with some continuing to be inhabited today. As Lloyd Kahn and Bob Easton record, 'Cappadocians carved entire cities, one to a depth of 265 feet, one an early 16 storey skyscraper. Two cities, one containing 20,000 people, were connected by a 6 mile long tunnel.'

Humans still live underground in the South Australian outback opal-mining town of Coober Pedy; in Matmata, a village in southern Tunisia; in China; and in the abandoned structures of New York and other major cities. Celebrated designer, writer, and TV presenter Kevin McCloud focused an entire *Grand Designs* programme on the contemporary renovation of an 800-year-old cave in the UK.

3. Ancient cone houses in Cappadocia, Turkey.

The shape of home

Situated as we are within our own era, it is easy to lose sight of the fact that the ways in which houses are built and used as homes shifts significantly over time. Early dwellings in diverse cultures were shelters where an undivided interior space was simply shared by all who resided or visited there, or else apportioned among different families. Activities such as socializing or meeting, conducting business, cooking, eating, and functions such as storage were assigned to public areas. As cultures developed and humanity dispersed around the globe, life got ever more complicated, and people's economic, political, and social roles became more differentiated. Many of these dynamics then came to be reflected in the ways in which houses are laid out and rearranged to reflect social status, but also to suit changing needs and tastes. So, for example, the hall that was once more or less identical to the home in medieval and Renaissance Europe and Britain has today become merely a transit zone into the inner space of the house, where the action now is. (It might be observed, however, that contemporary 'open plan' designs hark back in a way to the hall of medieval and earlier houses.) The living room that was once merely a formal space for entertaining special guests has given way to a place for family togetherness, relaxation, and entertainment (and where the entry hall has been banished, the outer door may lead straight into the living room). The hearth may now be a modern gas fireplace or it may be absent altogether. Toilets have moved from outside in the bushes or hanging off the edge of a house (or cliff) to a prominent place within, often as part of a showcase bathroom. (Bathrooms as we know them today were impossible before certain ancient civilizations, like the Minoans and later the Romans, learned how to pipe fresh water from distant sources. The flush toilet, invented in 1597, only came into common use in the mid-19th century.) Bedrooms—which in the more distant past didn't exist at all as distinct units—have morphed into private spaces where younger occupants are pretty much self-sufficient, as they assert their identities and explore the Internet, social media, and video games, and where older occupants play out their intimate lives.

Nor are these simple, smooth, one-way developments: witness the laundry room and kitchen. Whereas there was no laundry room for most people in past centuries, clothes having to be washed outside, elsewhere by paid launderers, or in communal settings (like riverbanks), the laundry room eventually moved inside into its own dedicated space. But in developed countries it is increasingly reduced to a pair of stackable machines cunningly fitted into an auxiliary nook or closet. Open-fire cooking areas were once located inside the living shelter, with a mere hole in the roof (or *oculus*) to exit smoke. With the invention of chimneys many centuries later, it became possible to have proper kitchens. However, the kitchen began life as a setting of drudgery, either completely separate from the house or, in wealthier dwellings, placed below ground in the servants' area. It has slowly evolved to the extent that now it is a gourmet chef's paradise, with all the latest gadgetry, and has been transformed by the miracles of modern materials and design into a focal point of domestic achievement and socializing. (The larder, once an indispensable adjunct to the kitchen, has long since been rendered nearly obsolete—as has the word itself—by refrigerators and freezers.)

In addition, attics, which formerly were empty, uninsulated, dead spaces, forlorn and spooky, suitable only for storage, have relatively lately been harvested for extra bedrooms and studies.

This brief glimpse of the domestic past and present indicates that the ways in which people utilize and arrange rooms within their living space says a good deal about how they visualize and evaluate their own (or others') houses as homes, and about the dominant cultural values of their time and place. The layout, function, and serviceability of the house has become ensconced in the idea of 'what a home should be' and of how it is called to mind, identified with, and (metaphorically) 'worn'.

Traces of what once was

Every house, except for those being occupied for the first time, has a history as a home or series of homes. Some residents find this fact interesting and desire to know more about those who've lived there in the past. Others seemingly have no such curiosity, instead regarding their own arrival as a clean slate on which to inscribe their homes' identities. This latter sensibility is acted out by renovating, repainting, redecorating, building extensions, introducing amenities, and filling the house with their chosen furniture and personal possessions.

Among those who feel the importance or weight of their dwelling's history will be those who experience 'ghosts of the past'. A smaller number of people will literally believe in ghosts (benign, mischievous, or malicious) that haunt the premises (Box 3). However, for most, this notion simply signifies an awareness that different lives have been led there, births and deaths have occurred, laughter and anger have flickered in these rooms, and other homey settings have been laid out within the same spaces over time.

There may be fantasies or everyday imaginings of these events, and little glimmers or signs of them may be uncovered, such as remnants of wallpaper or artifacts left behind, or evidence of how certain areas were utilized. Anecdotal accounts by neighbours, and articles and photographs in local newspapers can also fill in details.

Are houses more durable than homes? Physically, perhaps, but otherwise the answer is not so clear. An Australian woman, interviewed after extensive flood damage to her house had left her 'devastated', affirmed with emotion that 'This is my home. This is

> **Box 3 A ghostly presence may be felt in any home**
>
> The unhomelike, whatever its exact nature, attaches with some regularity to houses themselves. Sooner or later, doesn't everyone meet a haunted house? Someone dies. There is a divorce, or a child leaves home. And the rooms left behind are filled with that singular presence and baffling disappearance. I'm thinking of how, after my grandfather died, my grandmother stacked clean laundry on his side of the bed, his heavy watch dangling always from her wrist. Or say the childhood home must go on the block, its ancient keepers no longer able to clean the gutters and mow the lawn. How strange to see the place divested of its long-accustomed family life, that indescribable flavor boiled away; how much stranger, how appalling, really, to watch it fill promiscuously with the life of some other family. They chop down the gnarled old crab apple tree. They gut the kitchen. Their bicycles clutter the driveway. How do we bear it?
>
> (Katharine Greider, *The Archaeology of Home*, pp. 69–70)

not my house. This is my home. Twenty-two years...' Even among the ruins of one's place and possessions, there is a sense of home as an ongoing entity.

Many sorts of dwellings make one world

Houses made from natural materials, such as mud, wattle and daub (which includes animal dung), thatch, adobe, stone, clay, hand-made bricks, unprocessed or scrap wood, driftwood, reeds, bamboo, rammed earth, hay bales, and cedar shakes and shingles are found across a wide swath of the world—from Ireland and Norway to Mexico, to Myanmar (Burma), Samoa, and Japan. Many are freestanding, some are built into hillsides or constitute domed hills of their own. While these are often made by sustainable methods, rising populations in various locations may threaten supplies of traditional materials.

With increasing numbers of people moving to urban centres, housing shortages are rife across the globe. The solution that often arises, in cities as diverse as Calcutta, Ankara, and Nairobi, is the construction of squatter settlements, built from materials that are inexpensive or available for scavenging. Paul Oliver, a specialist in vernacular architecture (building designs devised by ordinary, untrained people), writes that a great deal of this housing is 'peripheral, makeshift, marginalized, self-built from urban detritus and perpetually threatened with demolition'.

But even when housing initiatives try to address accommodation shortages in an egalitarian fashion, the results may be dismal, with residents ending up being trapped in ghettos from which there is little chance of escape. In the 1800s, Benjamin Disraeli lamented the 'dreary repetitious mediocrity' of London's Victorian-period row houses. A century later, the same critique resurfaces in singer-songwriter Malvina Reynolds's satirical tune depicting the houses of 20th-century American suburbia as 'little boxes made of ticky tacky' that 'all look just the same' (and whose occupants—'doctors and lawyers and business executives'—are equally alike).

Wanderers

Although people around the world are increasingly on the move today, some groups always have been. Agriculturalists have been able to become sedentary, remaining more or less permanently in the same place. By contrast, nomads, responding to different demands of environment and livelihood, have built temporary or transportable structures for centuries. As Dan Frank Kuehn recounts,

> Nomadic sheep and yak herding communities migrate from the
> mountains to the plains in the fall, and back to the mountains in

the spring, following the grass for their grazing animals. Over the course of a year, a *ger* [more commonly known as a *yurt*] may be moved as many as nine times, in a lifestyle that enables these people to thrive in the farthest reaches of Outer Mongolia, where even the summers are cold.

One to five camels or oxen will carry a collapsed *ger* and all its furnishings, depending on the size of the family. It's said that in Genghis Khan's day, huge *gers* (over 20 feet in diameter) were pulled, fully assembled on wheeled platforms, across the Gobi Desert by twenty or more oxen.

Mobile homes are also used, or have been used, by societies and sub-cultures as diverse as the Roma people (Gypsies), the Touareg of Algeria, the Bedouin of North Africa and the Middle East, the Fulani of Niger, the trailer park residents of North America, the retired 'grey nomads' of Australia, and the houseboat residents of the Netherlands, Thailand, the US, India, and other countries. Thus, movable housing may represent a necessity, an inheritance from previous generations, or an alternative lifestyle choice.

In the past and present, many other wanderers come and go as well, some with and some—like the winter Florida-bound Canadians known as 'snow geese'—without their own portable accommodation. Wanderers have added greatly to the colourfulness of human history. Those who come to mind include: street entertainers and transient performers of various types plus their retinues (minstrels, troubadours, buskers, picture show men, thespians, carnies, and pugilists, to name a few); crusaders, mendicant priests, knights questing after the Holy Grail, travelling salesmen, merchants and traders, missionaries, mercenaries, ranch hands for hire, and roaming pastoralists. That some or all of these people have a keen sense of home, even though they generally lack a fixed residence, cannot be ruled out. Many evidently do, identifying with the land or thinking of home as comprising a life of meaningful travels.

Outlooks and inlooks

Dwellings express an 'outlook' or vantage-point, defined by various attitudes towards life. They possess an 'inlook' too: doors generally open inward, which is not only more convenient for the person entering, but also serves as a sign of welcome. Interior decor often speaks volumes about a building's occupants (see Chapter 5). Iconoclastic and eccentric builders construct all manner of dwellings. On Canada's Vancouver Island, Bruno Atkey designed a house, part of which is entered through a tree trunk; 'Margaret's Cabin', a small forest house on the same island, by Jan Janzen, 'was built almost entirely from a cedar tree that had been lying nearby'. The tree opened, symbolically, to reveal the house lying latent within (in a way reminiscent of Michelangelo's perception that sculptures residing in great pieces of marble silently await liberation by the sculptor). And then, as if by magic, an enclosure was created that brought the outside in, making for Margaret what is essentially a home in a tree.

Windows inevitably invite the outside in as well, but they may stare at facing windows nearby or merely confront a stark wall across an empty alleyway. Some are never cleaned, which may be the fault of the building management rather than the tenant, in the case of an upper-floor apartment. Windows may embrace and celebrate the outside, or they may shun it by being always curtained, shuttered, or designed for disuse.

In a watercolour painting by Cynthia Allman (see Figure 4), the window is a central, affirmative feature. The room she depicts is orderly, but not prissy. Relative affluence is evident and favourite things are displayed everywhere: plants, books, antiques, bric-a-brac. A book lies open, upside down on top of the bookshelf, and a self-satisfied cat of leisure snoozes on the stuffed chair, hinting that the artist has recently left the room, perhaps in

4. *Protected Area.*

5. 'Family in room in tenement house, ca. 1910'.

response to what looks like a letter, placed on the covers of the open book. The scene outside cannot be determined, but sunlight streaming through the window illuminates the room brightly, conveying an uplifting feeling and drawing the viewer willingly into the room. The artist celebrates the day and the comforts of a special place in which she spends her time.

By way of contrast, we can examine a photograph by Jacob A. Riis of a family at home in a New York tenement around 1910 (see Figure 5). Riis, who was himself a poor Danish immigrant in 1870, was the author of *How the Other Half Lives: Studies Among the Tenements of New York* (1890) and additional works, in which he visually captured the character of tenement life around the turn of the century. Riis was a pioneer in the use of flash photography, and one wonders how dim this scene would have appeared without it. Family members have put on their best attire and project an air of dignity in the cramped quarters they call home,

44

but one can detect the weight of what it must have been like just to get by financially. Cooking pots show up in the lower left corner, indicating that this room also serves as a kitchen. The stove would have burned wood or coal. There would have been no private toilet, and likely no running water (certainly no hot water); heating would have been provided by a fireplace; electric lighting would probably have been found only in the stairwells; little or no daylight would penetrate the inside. There would not even be a view, and the mental outlook would probably be apprehensive yet determined. In many such rooms, numerous people had to sleep together, and some were used by day as workplaces to help make ends meet. It is scarcely any wonder that there was so much street life at that time, given what things were like inside gloomy, dark rooms that were cold in winter and roasting in summer.

A quite different kind of interior is shown in Figure 6, which opens to view one room in a private house in Ladakh, a region in the mountainous north of India. A small window in the background is covered, but there is an unidentified source of warm light coming from the right side of the photograph. The main thing that impresses itself upon us is that this is a carefully tended, dedicated prayer room containing an ornate altar, and that someone is in the process of using it for a religious observance. The fact that this home includes such a room, and that the room is extensively decorated and obviously occupies a prominent position within the dwelling, tells us that religious beliefs and practices (in this case, of the Buddhist faith) play a central role in the lives of the home's occupants. Probably nothing in their daily routine is more important, and religion influences all levels of decision-making, just as it has in many geographically diverse societies of different periods.

The question of outlook and inlook was carefully probed by American architect Frank Lloyd Wright. Wright did not build average houses for average people; he built stunning, unprecedented houses for exceptional patrons of the art of

6. Prayer room in private home, Ladakh, India.

integrated home design. And he was a master at bringing the outside in. Architectural features such as large windows, breezeways, verandahs, courtyards, balconies, and wide openings onto outdoor gardens generally have this effect. But Wright eclipses all of these by using designs that literally build around and give right of way to earthly features, exhibiting his philosophy (known as 'organic architecture') of creating harmony with the environment. In his house called Fallingwater, built in the US state of Pennsylvania in 1935 (and now a National Historic Landmark), Wright devised numerous methods that allow interior and exterior space to interpenetrate. Consider just one example:

> The fireplace hearth in the living room integrates boulders found on the site and upon which the house was built—ledge rock which protrudes up to a foot through the living room floor was left in place to demonstrably link the outside with the inside.... The stone floors are waxed, while the hearth is left plain, giving the impression of dry rocks protruding from a stream.

Another amazing creation, Massaro House, was inspired by Wright's original plans for a lakeside site in New York State. Completed posthumously in 2007, this luxury home has Wright's signature, cantilevered deck jutting out into the lake, and features boulders that almost literally come crashing through the walls into the kitchen.

In California, a rustic house by Bill Heick is simply built around an old-growth redwood tree, which serves as its centrepiece and main support. In the US state of Washington, SunRay Kelley designs and constructs 'wildly imaginative...soaring, sculptural buildings' that rival, on a small scale, the fanciful creations of the great Spanish architect Antoni Gaudí. Kelley follows two mottos: 'I listen to Mother Nature; she's the boss' and 'The life spirit moves through us all the time.'

Homes as dwellings

An important question that might be raised in relation to this very brief and selective survey of dwellings is whether, and to what extent, all of these domiciles can be called 'homes'. It seems most reasonable (and egalitarian) to conclude that *all dwellings are homes and all homes are dwellings*, to one degree or another, and that they come in a great variety of types. Even a prehistoric cave, it could be argued, might have been a place of relative comfort, where some privacy was established in designated areas, and leisure family activities and the training of children took place in the intervals when other, more pressing outside activities were not being pursued. The same might be said of a traditional Iroquois longhouse or Plains First Nations earth lodge. But if a dwelling is a shelter in which people stay or reside for a while, where does this leave transient accommodation such as Inuit igloos; Lakota Sioux and Cheyenne tipis; Algonkian wigwams; !Kung San huts, made from plant materials; and Berber tents? For these nomadic and foraging peoples, the notion of home may combine identification with the land, where a traditional way of life is sustainable, with a sense that where you are is where you're meant to be at that time.

In her book *The Making of Home*, Judith Flanders distinguishes between 'home languages' spoken in certain countries and 'house languages' that hold sway in others. The former (English, Germanic, and Scandinavian tongues) have separate words for house and home, implying that a home is a particular type of entity around which life is organized, while the latter (Romance and Slavic languages) use the same word for both house and home, indicating that they are more oriented towards shared social space, and that home is less in need of being linguistically distinguished from house. This is an intriguing hypothesis, and certainly Flanders' project of tracing 'how homes came to be seen as special places' is an important and valuable one.

Bill Bryson also pursues this story in *At Home: A Short History of Private Life*. But he urges that 'wherever we go in the world we know houses and recognize domesticity the moment we see them. This aura of homeliness is, it turns out, extremely ancient.' Bryson's choice of example to underline the point is the neolithic village of Skara Brae in the Orkney Islands, off Scotland—'older than Stonehenge and the Great Pyramids, older than all but a handful of built structures on Earth'—which was first uncovered by a massive ocean storm in 1850. The residual houses in this settlement are still identifiable as homes that contain built-in stone dressers and beds, rudimentary plumbing, and locking doors.

Historical accounts and speculations about homes are fascinating and richly productive of useful knowledge. Yet above all, what we learn from them is that homes provide ways of connecting with each other, with our surroundings, and with the history of the place we are in. Humans have clearly evolved to be home-builders, home-makers, and home-nesters. So we come to the result that in spite of linguistic subtleties, architectural variations, and cultural specificities, homes are where people dwell, and they have been dwelling everywhere for as far back as we can trace or imagine.

Chapter 4
Remembering, imagining, and other mindwork

Reviving the past

It could be said that your childhood home—like anything else from earlier parts of your life—is just what you remember it to be, nothing more nor less. But is this really the whole story? First of all, there may be a flood of emotions associated with your memories of home. Second, memory is capable of distortion and disintegration (it 'plays tricks on us')—but sometimes acts of recollection 'untrick' us as well, by becoming clearer or fuller over time. This happens when suppressed or unrecalled items later resurface, either spontaneously or with effort, and this event may arouse feelings in addition to, or in place of, those we had before. So it seems that the act of remembering home may be variable in both content and impact from one point in time to the next; and, therefore, that memories of home are not set in stone. Marcel Proust's childhood memories, unleashed by the experience of eating a small cake called a *petite madeleine*, are delightfully described in the first volume of his monumental novel *Remembrance of Things Past*. And yet Proust, who wrote more about memory than perhaps any other novelist who ever lived, is the first to admit that acts of remembrance may not reveal what they appear to. So memory is elusive. Attempts to recall sometimes yield routine and completely expected results; but at other times a gain or loss in content or feeling is what we register instead.

Home may not be as good as we remember, but it may not be as bad either. Is home therefore merely an illusion of arbitrary or faulty recollection? No, because to start with, memories are *of* something. Furthermore, there are *facts* about the past, and these—like all facts—deserve respectful treatment. This suggests that there must be ways to get at the truth of the past. But how can one check the accuracy of recall? The answer is given to a certain extent by photographs, written communications we have saved, documents, the testimony of witnesses (neighbours and those who lived with or visited you), and the consistency of the things we reminisce about. It has to be admitted, though, that it is impossible in principle to test a memory by comparing it to the thing it purports to describe. We take a lot on trust about our own consciousness, as do others who interact with us (and vice-versa). And the narrative of our lives that we construct for ourselves is an ongoing project subject to revision at any time. This means that the past as we see it is always open to reinterpretation, quite apart from the issue of the factual accuracy of our memories.

Nostalgia

Nostalgic sentiments magnify these problems considerably. Nostalgia is defined as '1. a bittersweet longing for things, persons, or situations of the past; 2. the condition of being homesick; homesickness'. This feeling is actually quite complex. Notice that it is described as 'bittersweet'. The reason for this, presumably, is that we might *think* the past was better or simpler or easier to manage than the present, but we also aren't completely convinced that we would really want to trade 'then' for 'now', and know we couldn't even if we wanted to. What if you did succeed in going back in time? Would the past and the entities that populated it (such as the family home) really resemble what you now think about them? You have changed, after all. But also, since the past is frozen in time, you would only be a detached observer, nothing more. (You couldn't be an active agent or you'd be able to change the past.)

We might suppose that nostalgia is one thing, embellishment and romanticizing another. But this may not be the case. If we're overly drawn to the past by thoughts and feelings of lament and yearning, this is because of a lack experienced in the present. People do try to cling to a world that is gone when they recreate house styles of the past, seek out vintage clothing and retro furnishings, or perpetuate old-fashioned values. However, we know, in our heart of hearts, that the task of life is to deal with the situation we are actually in *now*, not one we believe we might prefer. We also need to be moving *forward* in our thinking and our lives. Nevertheless, as teacher Stephen Shaw observes, 'On occasions there seems to be a need to return, if only in our own minds, to times in which we imagined we were more secure, more protected, at peace with the world and ourselves.' And, at least for some of us, we probably were.

Returning home

The earlier discussion raises the issue whether anyone can ever go home, not just in memory but also as an act of recovery of some kind. This is much debated. 'The old place is exactly as I remember it', someone might say. But is it really? Could it possibly be? 'No matter where I go or return from, it'll always be the old family home.' Will it? We have to take such claims with a huge grain of salt. First of all, as noted earlier, memories of past events are selective, and they often grow unreliable with the passage of time. Second, things don't stay the same, owing to human intervention and natural processes of change, such as weather-caused wear and tear. Third, what happens when the family and nearby friends are gone, the contents moved, the premises sold and re-occupied or perhaps abandoned? Only a building and memory-pictures are left then. Fourth, we may be remembering what was gathered through a child's naive awareness; but now we are adults, with the senses, sensibilities, and emotional baggage of grown-ups. This last factor is the most interesting, if not also the most complicated to disentangle. For what we experience *now* has an overlay of what we remember experiencing *then*; and the activities of imagination and emotion are extremely difficult to disentangle from what we experience in the present moment, when sorting through our personal past. We can't divorce memory from our other mental faculties quite as easily as we might assume.

The majority view seems to be that you *can't* go back home in a meaningful and fulfilling way, or in a way that is true to yourself. Thomas Wolfe's novel *You Can't Go Home Again* makes this point as conclusively as possible in its very title. Wolfe's protagonist George Webber, himself a novelist, has thought deeply about life, endured its high and low moments, had deep and significant relationships, lived in at least three different countries, and has risen from obscurity to fame during the course of the narrative. Webber returns to the title theme several times in the novel. Once, when paying a visit to his old hometown, he observes that 'he never had the sense of home so much as when he felt that he was going there. It was only when he got there that his homelessness began.' Several hundred pages later, toward the end of the book, we learn that, 'The phrase [you can't go home again] had many implications for him.... In a way, the phrase summed up everything he had ever learned.'

Composer Philip Glass reflects similarly in his memoir *Words Without Music*. Describing the time when he moved away from his parents' house to attend university in Chicago, Glass says, 'I knew I had completely outgrown Baltimore and I was ready to pack a few bags and leave my childhood, family, and home behind to begin my "real life" (whatever that was).' Especially remarkable is the confidence Glass feels in recalling that his as-yet-only-potential 'real life' would prove to be more worthwhile than the life he had cast off. Wolfe's character Webber, although fictional, makes a summary judgement about home based on an entire life, whereas Glass closes the door on his home and past at a passing moment.

In the title piece of her short story collection *The Hidden Light of Objects*, Lebanese author Mai Al-Nakib portrays Zaina, a Kuwaiti mother, returning home after being held captive in Iraq for a decade (likely as a result of the 1990–1 Gulf War). Although her family has waited and hoped for this moment, and greeted her with love and joy, one of her adult children relates: 'We worry that our mother feels left out, a foreigner in her own home. *Unheimlich*, our father says to us and to her, a familiarity made uncanny, a home no longer homey.' And her welcoming family members all realize that 'There is no going back.' This feeling is confirmed by Zaina's own silent reflections. In spite of this, on encountering an old photograph of her husband and herself as young lovers, she perceives in it '*A promise to love, despite war and unrecoverable time. A way home*'. However, this is not a home she re-embraces so much as one that needs to be made anew, as an act of healing.

And yet...some have a strikingly opposite experience in which the original home *is* recovered. This (minority) viewpoint captures some of the best features of home—home as a secure place, even a sanctuary. Jessie Cole, an Australian novelist in her early 30s, lost her sister and father when still quite young—both having taken their own lives. Not long after, she had two babies and then became a single mother, with many raw wounds to heal. Declining the lure of the city (Brisbane and Melbourne), she chose to move back home: 'The pull of home was stronger.... For now, my home soothes me in a way nothing else can.... [H]ome has been my balm, my consolation.' This is clear testimony to the restorative power of home, notwithstanding the tragedies that have visited it, and representing, as it does here, the enveloping calmness of the familiar, where the roots of a person's particular history took hold and grew.

Returning to the family home while one's family or parents still live there may be a pleasurable occasion, but it also brings with it certain dilemmas, the most central of which is wondering—Where do I fit in now? Should I try to resume or revert to a role I played in the past when part of the close family circle or simply be myself, as I am today (and what does *that* mean, anyway)? What is my proper role there in the present moment? Certainly, there is an unspoken rule that I should assume some obligations and responsibilities, help out and participate, at least during the visit, as well as receiving the rewards of familiarity, affection, and togetherness. But what else is it appropriate or necessary for me to do or be?—No generalizations about these things will work for everyone.

A variation on the theme of returning home is found in expressions of faith in a 'heavenly home' that is more real and fulfilling than the 'vale of tears' we now live in. On this view, the present world is but a way station on the road to the hereafter. Embedded deeply within Christianity, Islam, and other religions, the idea is poetically expressed by different cultures. A proverb from Benin has it that 'The world is a journey, the afterworld is home.' Traditional African-American spirituals contain lines like: 'I've got a home in Beulah Land,/Outshines the sun./Way beyond the sky', 'Swing low, sweet chariot./Comin' for to carry me home', and 'Deep River,/My home is over Jordan'. This thirst for a home somewhere far away—'That promised land,/Where all is peace' ('Deep River')—has sustained many people through the worst hardships life has to offer.

Homes as symbolic expressions

Both internally and externally, homes express various meanings, beliefs, and attitudes, and convey messages about wealth, power, poverty, and other matters. Theologian Brian Walsh comments that domiciles in many cultures are imbued with 'symbols that remind the inhabitants of the founding story and guiding worldview that makes this place into home', and adds that home as such 'is a site of culturally meaningful and shared symbols'. Homes are symbolic in two ways: they communicate from within, by virtue of their patterns of placement, construction, and use; and they are interpreted from without, according to certain presuppositions and perspectives. Symbolic meanings are thus built into homes and also projected onto them. These two reference points are blended together as often as not. Hence, a house design may embody a belief system that governs the home it encloses, but it may acquire extra meanings over time that were not originally intended.

The now well-known 'upstairs, downstairs' layout of the British Edwardian-period (1901–14) townhouse was characterized in the television saga, *Downton Abbey*. Named after the house, the drama portrays this domestic arrangement, although in a countrified rather than urban setting. A less well-known 2002 'reality TV' series, *The Edwardian Country House*, offers another treatment of the theme. 'Upstairs' was occupied by a family of comfortable means, who owned the property, possessed entitlements and high social standing, and employed lower class help, upon which they were totally dependent. 'Downstairs' was the place where the servants went about their business, which was of course to tend to all the needs of their 'superiors' upstairs. This hierarchy of life activities represents, as a vertical spatial structure, the class system prevalent at that time and place, with the separation of classes and their work and pastimes being quite rigidly adhered to. Many servants, even if subjected to long hours of drudgery and not always well-treated, would not have questioned prevailing social divisions, and would have considered themselves lucky to be so employed, given that the poor of London and other big cities, scrabbling for a living, accounted for about a quarter of the overall British urban population.

Not only can the construction and uses of a house reinforce social distinctions, they may also reinforce gender differences. Who could fail to notice the messages conveyed by designating individual rooms, past or present, as 'master bedroom' or 'powder room'; or by carving up domains within the home along sex-specific and functional lines (explicitly or implicitly) as either male ('smoking room', 'billiards room', 'office') or female ('kitchen', 'laundry', 'nursery'). In many Arab Muslim countries, according to architecture and planning scholars Eman Abdelrahman Farah and Björn Klarqvist, interior spaces are similarly gender-specific (for example, male and female courtyards), and more generally divided up into 'the family/female domain and the male/visitor domain'—although both kinds of functional space are equally well-integrated into the house's structure as a whole. Farah and Klarqvist point out that this design simply applies an Islamic scriptural injunction to respect privacy. They add that 'there is nothing mentioned in the Koran about the seclusion or segregation of the female in the house or anywhere else'.

Those who are rich often live in the hills surrounding a city, where the views are better, the centres of commerce and industry are at a distance and can be avoided and compartmentalized off from one's conscious awareness, and which cost more to build in. Here, location (which real estate agents assure us is 'everything') very plainly expresses the owners' social rank. There are notable exceptions, however, such as Rio de Janeiro and Caracas, where the poor populate the hillsides. Both cities have their wealthy neighbourhoods, however—Rio's being by the sea and Caracas, situated inland, with its affluent population living in lower altitude, urban areas.

Polynesian peoples were observed in the 18th and 19th centuries to have houses that reflected the status of their occupants in subtle ways. In Tahiti, Jerry Moore states, 'the size and layout of houses were distinct for elites and commoners...Such differences were indicated by house posts....The houses of elites and the buildings used in rituals had posts carved from breadfruit wood; the lower status dwellings did not.'

Looking elsewhere, the Pawnee First Nations people of the Central Plains, US, constructed earth lodges with a circular floor plan representing the Earth and a domed roof echoing the sky. The walls and entrance of this dwelling were faced so as to honour the important stars and planets that were central to their cosmology. For example, the door faced the Morning Star (Mars), which stood for 'light, warmth and male power', while the back wall, within which the home's altar was situated, pointed in the direction of the Evening Star (Venus), signifying 'female power, creation and renewal of life'.

Neolithic, Bronze Age, and Iron Age peoples of Europe accorded religious significance to their homes. As Moore explains, 'offerings were made before a house was constructed and after a house was abandoned. The very process of building a home and the home itself became intertwined in ritual.' Cultures as distant from one another as ancient Egyptians, prehistoric peoples of the Andes region of Peru, and Neolithic residents of Çatalhöyük in Anatolia (now Turkey) structured their houses to take account of burying the dead beneath and within their walls. Figuratively as well as in fact, the departed had home ties preserved, which not only manifested their continuing presence for the living but also served to safeguard the future lives of the dead, whatever they might be.

Among ancient cultures such as the Alaskan Aleut and the Kayan of Borneo, hunting was often accompanied by elaborate rituals of purification and self-denial, involving temporary banishment from the home.

In customs surrounding the month of May or Midsummer, people in many parts of Europe (past and present) cut trees or branches for their villages, with which to bless their shared living place, individual homes, or both.

Cherokee First Nations tribes of the southeastern US lived in settlements that featured a 'townhouse'. This was a large but separate version of the houses they themselves occupied, so that it resembled individual dwellings, and vice-versa. The symbolic and practical function of the townhouse was to create a sense of identity and community through the many events and activities held there, reinforced by the linked structural details. Townhouses contained 'a sacred and eternal fire', but were also regularly renewed by being burnt down and rebuilt, always on the exact same spot. Communal buildings exist in many parts of the world—but this situation, where homes symbolically gain membership of a larger whole by being small-scale facsimiles of a shared town hall, appears unprecedented.

Sir James George Frazer relates, in his wide-ranging anthropological study *The Golden Bough*, that a ritual surviving into modern Greece featured the bloodletting and burial of animals beneath the foundation-stone of a new building to give it 'strength and stability'. The measure of a man's body or of his shadow might be used as an alternative tracing on which to set the base.

Feng Shui (*fung-shway*) is a cosmology that has garnered considerable attention and adherence in the West, although it has been known in China for millennia. Some of its basic ideas concern the placement, construction, interior design, and furnishing of the home and the activities that take place within it, as well as the layout of the outside garden space. Briefly, Feng Shui (meaning 'wind and water') is a philosophy that focuses on the energy (*qi*, or 'chi') that is believed to animate everything in the world, and that operates according to principles that must be followed within the home in order to enhance the quality of one's health and personal life more generally. So the goal is to set up the home and live in it in ways that harmonize with the flow of energy through it and beyond. In order to do this, it is necessary to avoid constrained spaces in home design, to position objects in certain ways, and to choose appropriate colour schemes for different parts of the house that correspond to various aspects of life.

Modern houses that are built from 'green', 'environmentally friendly', or recycled materials and have high insulation ratings, solar panels, internal gardens, and carefully planned natural surroundings make a statement, as of course do houses without these elements. The former 'announce' a commitment to energy efficiency, renewable energy sources, maintaining a smaller 'ecological footprint', being 'closer to nature', and the like. While these values were once defined as 'alternative' and 'countercultural', they have now become more mainstream. But we could also say that Western civilization, to the extent that it is moving in this direction, is reinventing the wheel, because many prehistoric peoples lived within a worldview that valorized a close relationship to the environment, and featured careful use and conservation of natural materials, an attitude of responsible stewardship, a sense of obligation to future generations, thrift, and related ideas.

Houses and other forms of dwelling are symbolic from the word go, then, in that much of what they stand for can be interpreted (or 'read-off') from their structural, functional, and decorative properties. A house can be infused with a variety of meanings; but we should avoid thinking that the symbolism of dwellings is immutable. And this is where we begin to encounter the interpretive symbolism of the home, introduced from an external perspective.

Sometimes home symbolism involves the overlay of meanings that are mainly products of the imagination. A case in point from Western culture is the gothic mansion styled as a 'haunted house'. This sort of abode symbolizes danger, mystery, fear of the unknown, and the omnipresent possibility of death. Its inhabitants are themselves considered weird and vaguely threatening. These features are responsible for the attraction/repulsion attitude with which the filmgoer or novel reader apprehensively engages with the house. In other cultures, voodoo, witchcraft, or black magic yield the fear factor that is projected onto the dwelling. But a cleansing ritual or a fresh coat of paint, redesign of the interior, some pest control, a bit of landscaping, and new tenants may dispatch the haunting altogether.

Different people occupying the same living space in different eras may have their own distinct symbolic agendas—as may those residing together. These can create conflict, for example between cohabiting individuals. Hence, disharmony over the home is often a symptom rather than a cause of deeper forms of strife. One member of a couple may perhaps see the quarters they jointly occupy merely as a unit of investment, while for the other, it may represent the protective nurturing of childhood. Or they might hold split views on the importance of using the home to display, for example, their affluence or ethnicity.

The dream home

Two of the great founding figures of psychoanalysis, Sigmund Freud and his protégé Carl Gustav Jung, were quite committed to interpreting the house from the standpoint of dream symbolism. Freud maintains that in dreams, the human body is commonly represented as a house. He offers examples from German of how this symbolism is also reflected in everyday language. But it was Freud's rebellious erstwhile follower who took the dream symbolism of the house much further. Jung argues that the dream-representation of the self as a house is a repeating phenomenon with profound roots of meaning in the human psyche. We do not invent this symbolism, he says, but rather we inherit it from the past—from the 'collective unconscious', the level of the mind where humans are on an equal footing, regardless of time and culture. The dream state presents the symbol as a motif that can, in turn, be utilized in psychoanalysis as a tool to promote greater self-understanding.

Freud later speculated that from the earliest times, houses have symbolized the womb, a place of safety to which we would return if we could. While this intriguing idea has been embraced by some literary and artistic figures as well as some in the alternative health and spirituality movements, it has not gained as wide an acceptance as one might have expected.

Juxtaposed to the house as a symbolic presence within dreams is the dream house or dream home itself, which many cherish owning in their private inner world of fantasies, wishes, and wants. This may simply be a place, however humble, that one dreams of being able to afford some day. Or it may be envisioned as the ultimate or ideal home, the one that manages to realize all of one's desires and expectations, the one that ticks all the boxes for space, layout, function, decor, and so on. Alternatively, it might merely amount to a home where one can finally come to rest, away from the turbulence, temptations, and trials of the world. However it is viewed, the dream house is an expression of self, enhanced by imagination, in the mode of dwelling.

Home is also the subject of many of our daydreams. This can be a home of the past, one that was especially meaningful or important; one that we aspire to have; or just some ideas and images we are playing around with or exploring with a view to planning for the future. In these various ways, home can preoccupy and entertain us as an object of remembrance, idle entertainment, or serious intent.

Finally, from the perspective of today's international refugees, who may own nothing but the clothes on their backs and live in dehumanizing border camps or detention centres, the quest for freedom, work, safety, self-betterment, and a decent country in which to raise one's children may coalesce in the dream of a home—a coveted destination in which to settle, be safe, and be treated with respect and dignity (see Chapter 7).

Home psychology in retrospect

Reminiscing about home. Dreaming about home. Getting nostalgic about home. Wondering about that place where one grew up but has not seen for so long—What we put into our concept of home through acts of memory and imagination is an enormous part of what home means to us. For many, thinking about home is like tracing a vein of incredible metallic wealth. It leads on and on without any clear end-point.

We also learn from the examples taken up in this chapter that beyond the personal meanings of home space that resonate with different individuals, there may be, and often is, a broader nexus in which homes model, mirror, elaborate, symbolize, appropriate, and incorporate meanings from the world at large, or even the entire universe. In these ways, home is connected with larger spheres of existence and narrative, and cultural identity is established.

Chapter 5
People, objects, and identity

Identity and home

A person's identity or sense of self is a complex product of experiences, beliefs, personal interactions, behaviours, engagements with space and place, and attachment to things. These factors are shaped by emotional states, memory, and imagination, as we saw in Chapter 4. A major focal point for the construction of self-identity is the home. Psychiatrist James Yandell offers the following insight:

> Nesting, home-making is a major means of personal expression and development. We create our immediate environment and then contemplate it and are worked on by it. We find ourselves mirrored in it, see what had been not yet visible, and integrate the reflection back into our sense of self....A right home...can protect, heal, and restore us, express who we are now, and over time help us become who we are meant to be.

As children, we are dependent upon parents, siblings, and relatives to provide a stable environment in which to explore and define ourselves. When a 'right home' is denied us by poverty, conflict, circumstances of neglect or abuse, or by some other cause, painful and maladaptive personalities often result (Box 4).

Box 4 People carve out home space even within institutions

Sociologist David Wästerfors observes that '"home" as a word is often used to soften or hide non-home features of [youth care, penal, elderly care, and other] institutions'. Yet, he continues, 'Personal spaces, privacy, and integrity (or insisting on "being yourself" no matter what)' represent 'home practices in settings or situations where we might not expect them', and help residents feel they are 'making themselves a bit at home, even if living in institutions'.

(David Wästerfors, 'Fragments of home in youth care
institutions', pp. 132, 130–1)

A combat soldier in a far-off place longs for home—perhaps for the comfort and safety of a childhood/young adulthood space, his or her room. What does this individual long for? It isn't just an area of the house with certain measurements, a built-in closet, a door, two windows, and so on. It is a personalized space, existing at a simpler time, with valued belongings in it, that gives identity to the room as well as to him or her; and, through comforting memories, this provides some kind of escape from present reality while promising self-restoration in the future. Even under some of the most unfavourable conditions, people try to connect with an idea of home that they cherish.

Companion animals also make a home what it is for many people, whether they live in rural settings such as farms and villages, or in urban ones. (And wild, non-domesticated animals have their own homes—but that's another story.)

House and home

There is a strong tendency to identify house and home, and even to use the words interchangeably. But the distinction between the two is quite important to preserve. In the popular song 'A House Is Not a Home', written by Burt Bacharach and Hal David for a 1964 film of the same title, a fractured love affair leading to physical separation of a couple transforms their home into a mere house, a residence where the one who is abandoned and remains there goes through the motions of living but is unhappy and unfulfilled. Although the song is about a troubled relationship, the movie is actually inspired by the bestselling autobiography of Pearl 'Polly' Adler, a Russian Jewish immigrant to the United States who ran a lucrative brothel catering to New York gangsters and celebrities during the Prohibition and Depression eras. A house of this kind could never be a home for anyone, Adler observes, and nobody could disagree with her judgement.

We can intuitively see the truth in the statement: 'You can sell your house but not your home.' A home is always a house plus many other ingredients; a house is a home minus many elements. Philosopher Robert Ginsberg sums up this thought as follows: 'Our residence is where we live, but our home is how we live.' Therefore, when we focus too much on the house (or any dwelling structure) as the essence of home, we neglect the most important components: the interactions among people who live together (relationships) and their behaviour regarding the objects (possessions, mementos, artifacts, goods, commodities, and so forth) which fit out their home space. Complex qualities emerge from these interactions and evolve over time. In short, *home is an ambience created by those who live there* (Box 5).

Home as people who matter

For many of us, home is primarily those with whom we have grown up and/or spent significant periods of time in close proximity. Growing up is of course not merely a matter of getting bigger and older and physically more robust, but also entails developing mentally—gaining cognitive and emotional maturity, self-confidence, consolidation and validation of oneself as a

Box 5 Home is the subject of numerous cultural products

The urge to place ourselves within a homescape is abundantly manifested in cultural products. Examples include: Georgia O'Keeffe's paintings of the American Southwest and Emily Carr's canvases of the Canadian wilderness and First Nations coastal villages; the Czech composer Antonin Dvořák's Symphony No. 9 (*From the New World*) and great symphonic poems by Jean Sibelius (*Finlandia*) and Bohemian/Czech composer Bedřich Smetana (*The Moldau*); films like *Gone with the Wind*, *The Wizard of Oz*, *Cathy Come Home*, *E.T.*, *Heimat*, *The Castle*, *Finding Nemo*, and *99 Homes*; novels such as *Little Women*, *Cloud Street*, and *The Grapes of Wrath*; and popular TV shows like the *Little House on the Prairie* series, *Coronation Street*, *Neighbours*, *EastEnders*, *Everybody Loves Raymond*, *The Simpsons*, *A Place to Call Home*, *Resurrection*, and *Homeland*.

person, and a more 'worldly' outlook. People who are closest to us can help us reach this plateau.

The 'people' view of home is echoed by many voices, of which contemporary literature provides plentiful examples. In science fiction novelist Robin Hobb's book *Fool's Fate*, Fitz, a main character, simply asserts that 'home is people. Not a place. If you go there after the people are gone, then all you can see is what is not there anymore.' This statement illustrates the perspective we are considering in a fairly stark and one-sided manner. Fitz claims that the content of what home represents is exhausted by interpersonal relationships, and in addition, that what you can 'see' on returning home after its familiar occupants no longer reside there requires memory and imagination (seeing 'in the mind's eye', as we say).

Here we have another instance of the argument over what home means; but it is an argument in which we need not take sides.

Some think this way, some do not. Those who do may depend on the folks back home to affirm their identities in an active, ongoing way, which leads to a sense of loss or emptiness when they are no longer actively present in one's life. Others respect or at least acknowledge the influence of familial relationships, but are more independent in themselves. Yet we all experience being cut off from the past—our personal past—when grandparents, parents, or important siblings die; the past then becomes beyond reach in certain respects. Most of us also realize, however, that there are additional primary ingredients to home besides people, which we will get to in a moment.

Sometimes the idea that home is people (or another person) strikes one like an epiphany, sweeping away other seemingly durable attitudes towards belonging. In Stephanie Perkins's young adult novel *Anna and the French Kiss*, we encounter a case of this sort. Returning home to Atlanta after the beginning of a serious romantic encounter during a long stay in Paris, Anna Oliphant reflects on a phone conversation with her French boyfriend:

> And for the first time since coming home, I'm completely happy. It's strange. Home. How I could wish for it for so long, only to come back and find it gone. To be here, in my technical *house*, and discover that home is now someplace different.
>
> But that's not quite right either.
>
> I miss Paris, but it's not home. It's more like...I miss this. This warmth over the telephone. Is it possible for home to be a person and not a place?

A few lines later, Anna has made up her mind and succinctly answers her own rhetorical question: 'This is home. The two of us.' Such is the power of love, one might sigh. Again, we have a fairly exaggerated point of view, expressed as a radical psychological shift that transforms an individual's entire outlook on home. But the reorientation and new mental set is believable in terms of the change in self-identity that is taking place before our eyes.

For the protagonist of another popular fiction writer, Sarah Dessen,

> Home wasn't a set house, or a single town on a map. It was wherever the people who loved you were, whenever you were together. Not a place but a moment, and then another, building on each other like bricks to create a solid shelter that you can take with you for your entire life, wherever you may go.

The singularity of this perception comes from the notion that home is not a place at all, even though it has the durability of a 'solid shelter' made of bricks. The key image here is a metaphor suggesting that the story's character possesses an internalized and portable 'structure', which is the possibility of renewed encounter with 'the people who loved you' at any time and place. What counts most is the capacity for especially significant personal relationships to linger as a kind of living presence within the fabric of consciousness, reinforcing one's identity in an ongoing way.

These reflections on home are intriguing, but it is easy to be lulled into supposing that the idea of home as people who matter is freely constructed by us. In reality, however, quite dissimilar, more fixed, social formations of home exist in different cultures. For example, the Minangkabau of western Sumatra (Indonesia) are a matrilineal society that is Muslim, yet also blends into its belief system a nature philosophy known as *adat*. After marriage, a husband is expected to move with his wife into her mother's house and provide for her family without, however, having much decision-making power.

Another example concerns the Akan people of Ghana. Kobena Hanson, who has studied this culture, argues that Akans, like

Africans more generally, often live according to patterns that contrast markedly with those that prevail elsewhere.

> Conceptually, the household, with its connotations of coresidence, spatial enclosure, and common property, is a Western standard.... Residents of a house, especially the traditional compound house ... will, aside from core family members, include fostered children of relatives, inlaws (both paternal and maternal), fictive kin, and friends.... The result is a myriad of living arrangement forms. Common examples include, but are not limited to: (a) a group of individuals who live, eat, and sleep together under one roof; (b) a group of individuals who live and eat together, but sleep in separate residences under different roofs; (c) a group of individuals who eat together, but live and sleep in different residences; and (d) a group of individuals with a constituent member living, eating, and sleeping in a separate place, yet with all aspects of this person's livelihood taken care of by the group.

These various configurations should stimulate us to think about home more broadly—as having multiple locations, or a primary location, or no specific location, or as having an altogether different, culturally grounded meaning that needs to be experienced in order to be properly understood. The lesson here is to be on guard against using familiar kinds of relationships as the standard for making generalizations and for judging the unfamiliar—just as we saw in Chapter 1 that it is important not to rely too heavily on the English word for 'home' as a universal lens.

Home as a material environment

In addition to *people*, the *objects* that populate our homes contribute greatly to defining who we are. But it's not just that who we are is expressed in and by the things we own; our possessions also influence how our identities are shaped. And here we encounter the 'objects' view of home.

As we appropriate things in the natural world, they take on the roles we assign them in the human world. Modifying basic stuff so as to produce useful, not-so-useful, and purely aesthetic objects is a form of human activity we encounter everywhere. The truth of this can be seen across a wide range of cultures. It might be assumed that because sedentary cultures are accumulative, nomadic peoples (such as hunter-gatherers) are the opposite, having no possessions. This would be a mistake. Groups on the move obviously do not amass as much as settled ones and may be less defined by what they own, but they nevertheless have important things to transport: weapons for self-defence and hunting, digging tools, cooking utensils, ceremonial and religious objects, materials to protect against the weather, and objects of adornment and recreation, to name a few.

The pragmatic value of objects derives from their being fashioned or constructed from natural or invented materials so as to serve definite purposes and satisfy various desires. What is more striking, though, is the idea that objects literally create humans. On a certain level, this is plainly true. We need environmentally supplied nutrients to ingest, air to breathe, and water to drink in order to survive. All other human endeavours are contingent on this foundation. But the impact of objects on our lives goes much further, and an entire field of research—material culture studies—is devoted to this subject.

Each person can grasp the connection between objects and self-identity very directly. From the time we are children on to adulthood and old age, we accumulate things that matter to us and which we use to mark out a certain zone—or intimate domain—of our being. The things each of us possesses may vary widely in nature and significance, and do not necessarily always retain the same value for us, except perhaps within our memories of a particular stage of personal development. The 'intimate domain' that is specially mine or yours may be anything from a secret hiding place (or cubby or clubhouse) to a bedroom, library, hobby or collection display room, even a more public space within the house or adjacent to the house, such as a garden, gazebo, or pathway.

Humans have evolved in relation to things by trial and error, as the properties of objects help teach us how to be creative and what new technological advances are possible, what kinds of stuff are potentially harmful, and so on. Today, we coexist with many interactive and applied devices such as computers, smart phones, video games, 3D printers, navigational tools, and robotic prostheses, not to mention the relationships that are mediated (made possible and facilitated) by the hardware and software that underpin email and social media communication. These are all designed to enhance our lives, but they give feedback that modifies our behaviour in turn, enabling us to gain new pathways to knowledge, self-development, and effectiveness in gaining the results we seek.

Entire domains of human activity are shaped by material means and conditions. Commerce involves the exchange or sale of goods and things to satisfy demand; and the use of some kind of medium of exchange (money or another kind of tangible symbol) has become universal in these transactions. One can also think of music, painting and other art media, sports, the practice of technical skills, manufacturing, medicine, and travel—all pursuits that depend on certain objects in order to exist, and which also enable people to interact with one another in meaningful and important ways.

Geographer Yi-Fu Tuan observes that the living environment of humans is

> richly populated with particular and enduring things. The particular things we value may be given names: a tea set is Wedgwood and a chair is Chippendale....An object such as a valued crystal glass is

recognized by its unique shape, decorative design, and ring when
lightly tapped. . . . An object or place achieves concrete reality when
our experience of it is total, that is, through all the senses as well as
with the active and reflective mind.

Objects provide a kind of catalyst for people's reactions, and a
material language for conversing and interrelating. Tuan also
illustrates here the extent to which we rely on a stable arena of
objects in order to give our lives meaning and solidity.

There is as well the negative side of human dependency on things,
falling under the euphemistic heading of 'substances'. Alcoholism
and drug addiction are 'substance dependencies', and for some
unfortunate people, self-identity is difficult, if not impossible,
to detach from these objects of abuse. The ownership and
accumulation of objects is itself sometimes thought of as akin to
an addiction. Karl Marx, for example, claimed that the capitalist
economy has given rise to 'commodity fetishism'. The idea here is
that when manufactured objects acquire a market price, becoming
goods that can be bought and sold, we learn to think of them in
terms of their monetary value and to attribute that to the things
themselves. But in Marx's view, this conceals the fact that market
value really originates in the cost of the labour required to produce
things, which is in turn determined by the (exploitative)
relationship between capitalist and worker. To view consumer
products apart from this context, he holds, is to engage in
misrepresentation and mystification.

Other social critics have also suggested that many, perhaps most,
people live within a system in which they are in thrall to objects.
And indeed, we are all familiar with the notion of having too many
things and of being manipulated by advertising to embrace fads
and fancies of the moment. If we look around ourselves at what
we own and ever feel the need for 'spring cleaning' or 'downsizing',
we will doubtless encounter our own habits of excess.

Living with objects

For a long time and across many cultures, houses have served to announce to the world their occupants' lifestyle and social position. The house itself, as we have seen in Chapters 3 and 4, makes a statement about the status of its residents. This is not ordinarily thought of when the structure in question conforms to a traditional or modern plan, or has a mass-marketed, practical design. However, the state of its upkeep and how well the surroundings are developed and maintained inevitably have an impact on the image it projects. Houses that attract notice are generally more unique in appearance and built of higher quality or special materials, and therefore signify the economic means required to produce them. Status-enhancement may not be the primary intention behind a given piece of design and construction, but the house in question will likely serve that purpose as well as satisfying more mundane ends.

The objects selected to fill the interior space of a house, as sociologist Ian Woodward observes, are 'at once integrating and differentiating', by which it is meant, first, that 'they must be able to be decoded by people, in everyday practice, as embodying elements of a particular style, aesthetic mode or taste'. One can think here of designer versus Ikea kit furniture; original artwork versus reproductions; genuine imports with a pedigree versus mass-produced copies. And, second, the objects can at the same time make a statement about what is most personally valued by their owner, what is of special importance in her or his world, and which commodities are deemed essential. Neither the owner nor the onlooker can always be sure of the force of such 'statements', however. For example, do posters of Che Guevara, Bob Marley, or The Rolling Stones' lips-and-tongue logo still convey the ethos of rebellion, or has their original energy been sapped by commercial overexposure? And what remains today of the original significance of Shaker furniture: simplicity, honesty, and humility?

Objects and decor can likewise be utilized to advertise a 'look' or 'style' that is thought best suited to communicate what philosopher James Tuedio calls an 'orienting sense of home'. Look or style is clearly a culturally relative notion; a homeowner in Hong Kong may select Art Deco embellishments and furnishings, while one in the US may aim to create a Moroccan or Mexican mood. In this philosophy of home creation and improvement, the functional and/or purely aesthetic items that constitute the basic appearance of a room, if chosen with the utmost care, will be those that possess significant personal meaning, that affirm who one is or what one wishes to be seen as. This sounds like conspicuous wish-fulfilment and ego-projection, which is being carried out within the home by means of the transformation of its rooms and their contents. To a certain extent, it is. For in one's homey habits of self-expression, wants can become needs over time. As people grow more affluent, their activities, such as work, become less focused on obtaining the fundamental necessities of life and more directed to developing a lifestyle governed by focal interests, pleasure, comfort, and self-actualization—something that it appears people everywhere aspire to, regardless of their means.

Home and possessions: two examples from the Holocaust

The links between home, objects, and personal identity are dramatically illustrated by two stories centring on the Holocaust. The Nazis conducted widespread looting of Jewish homes and museums, in which precious artworks were confiscated. Allied troops liberating Europe discovered over 1,050 facilities where such works had been stored, and as many as 100,000 works in all were gathered up, many destined for Hitler's planned ultimate museum of art. These private possessions, including French Impressionist paintings, modernist works, paintings by old masters, and ancient artifacts, were highly valued by their owners, not only because of their rarity and significant monetary value, but also because they were aesthetically appreciated and outstandingly important in shaping their home environments. In 2012, more than 1,400 paintings were found in a private residence in Munich, many of which are believed to have been stolen by the Nazis. In addition, thousands of works designated as 'degenerate' or 'rubbish', according to the Nazi ideology, were publicly burned in 1939 in Berlin. Most people do not enjoy the luxury of owning famous artworks. But most do appreciate great art, and everyone has possessions of personal value and significance that should enable her or him to grasp the deep meaning that these works of art—especially those handed down through the generations—must have had for these people—their beloved property confiscated in illegal and discriminatory acts by those holding arbitrary power over them. Indeed, anyone who has experienced the personal violation felt as the result of a robbery or home invasion will find that this narrative of loss resonates all the more readily.

The second story concerns more mundane things. Beyond the special objects that we each own, there are the everyday objects we rely on to make a life. This includes household furnishings, cooking equipment, eating utensils, clothes, bedding, and all the other things we normally take for granted. These possessions are barely thought of as we go about our affairs—they form the silent but indispensable backdrop to our homes. And it turns out that the Nazis plundered such items as well—on a massive scale in France, Belgium, and the Netherlands—and had them sorted and meticulously catalogued by prisoners at work camps, taking the best for themselves and their cronies, and redistributing the rest to German civilians. Personal items such as photos and documents were burned. Any valuables, like pianos, porcelains, silverware, furs, and special fabrics, were similarly siphoned off. This astonishing process seems to have been implemented more to eradicate any sense of Jewish presence or reality than to supply others with precious or useful goods. It demonstrates that destroying homes and their occupants' ties to place also amounts to erasing things that mould identities and create networks of memories.

The power of objects

Holocaust events disclose many unhappy truths about exploitation and victimization, about dehumanization and the premeditated cruelty of which humans are capable. These two stories also illuminate, in a striking and tragic manner, the part played by a home's contents, apart from other factors that constitute it. When a home is emptied, it becomes a shell, a mere house, and loses its homeyness. In forced expulsions, it forfeits its identity, as the people whose home it was become the hidden dispossessed, mere numbers and pawns in a larger game the outcome of which they cannot hope to influence.

We experience here a confronting realization of the capacity objects have to fashion our identities within the context of a home. Personal objects, such as mementos, photographs, letters, emails, souvenirs of a place or occasion, and heirlooms have special meaning to us. What is not so immediately apparent is that absolutely ordinary objects—the fixtures, movables, and humble implements of daily life—register here too. What is common to both the personal and the everyday is a history of use and function, the role these things played and continue to play in our individual and group activities. This may be either an occasional role, as in the use of the finest china for festive gatherings, or a regular use, such as is provided by living room sofas, beds, mirrors, clothing, and laptops. Objects have the potency they have because we use them all the time, they were chosen by us and reflect our taste, and they represent a large component of what makes our house into a home. Some things are of little or no importance to anyone else, but of great value to oneself—for example, photos taken in a coin-operated booth, ticket stubs from a beloved concert event, an embossed paper napkin from a friend's wedding, a souvenir pin from one's travels. In each case, the objects concerned stand out because they tell a story; or to put it in more contemporary terms, they fit into a life-narrative, namely, your own.

Chapter 6
Home politics

Politics as inescapable

Politics, it might be said, is everywhere—in interactions between and within groups, between groups and individuals, and among individuals—and the term applies to situations ranging from cooperation, mutual respect, and equal participation to exploitation, abuse, and disenfranchisement. Even homelessness has a political dimension (see Chapter 7). Specifically, politics refers to the processes and strategies people use to obtain what they want. It also concerns the outcomes and social structures that result and their influence, in turn, on shaping people's everyday lives. Home politics affects anyone who lives with other people, because transforming a space into a home involves negotiations of various sorts. Wherever people live together, there is bound to be a regime for gaining power and advantage, or agreeing to share them. Sometimes the energies and structures that flow from these arrangements are evident to us, sometimes not. We can always benefit, though, from trying to make what is political a bit more transparent.

Public and private life

A popular slogan from the 1960s and 1970s was that 'the personal is political'. This means that the boundary between the public and private spheres is indistinct at best, and that issues and dynamics traditionally supposed to be confined to the former cross over into the latter and are replicated there, but also the reverse. People's private lives, and their relationships to those with whom they cohabit, are subject to many influences originating in the public sphere. Government regulations, such as laws concerning norms of sexual conduct, what counts as a legitimate marriage, reproductive rights, and gender equality, have a major impact on the way people's private lives are conducted, as well as their quality of life. And in a reverse motion, when people vote according to their beliefs, they project and affirm their privately held opinions and values in the space of public life.

Social norms, tendencies, and attitudes are likewise relevant here. So, for example, if the rights of women and children are non-existent or routinely subordinated to those of men, then it can be expected that power relations within the home will mirror this reality. As Juliet Williams, a professor of law and society and women's studies, puts it, 'the public/private distinction can create a sanctuary for oppression'.

Those who challenge the status quo within their private lives may find themselves up against conditions set by the law or determined by social norms and prevailing attitudes. This will lead them to feel isolated and in need of uniting with others in the struggle to change these forms of behavioural control. In this process they will be acting out their private lives within the public sphere. But it could be maintained that we all do this anyway, in one manner or another, depending on whether we adhere to legal and social expectations in our intimate dealings with each other, or else choose to pursue new and different, 'game-changing' kinds of relationships. Sometimes, however, occupancy of a home may not only be an assertion of the right to equality and equal treatment, but also of who one really is. Thus, geographer Sarah

Ellwood, writing of 'lesbian living spaces', argues that 'home is a place where members of a minority group become subject rather than object', a context in which one 'assumes the right to be entirely open about her identity'.

The home and beyond

Edwin Heathcote notes that gas, water, and electric utilities, as well as sewage effluent, connect the private space of the house with public space, making a home dependent on what is outside of it. The public/private boundary is blurred and crossed over many times daily by electronic technologies as well. First radio and then television brought a flood of information and opinions into the home, influencing how people think about the world and events happening elsewhere. Now, with multiple TV sets not uncommon, with computers having revolutionized our lives once again, and with virtually everyone owning a smart phone, entertainment areas in the home are decentralized, leading to a greater emphasis on developing private spaces such as individuals' bedrooms and studies. In more affluent homes today, a dedicated theatre room is often present too. Heathcote further observes that modern transmission technology enables the home to have 'a literal connection with the cosmos, receiving rays from satellites in outer space: an absolutely extraordinary idea yet one perhaps commensurate with the dominance of the TV screen in our rooms as a surrogate window to the world'. In recent years, both governments and businesses have begun gathering information on people's phone, email, and Internet use records from within their homes. Many find this political intrusion objectionable and yet it seems inescapable. In a multitude of ways, then, the public sphere invades and defines the private—and interprets for us the actualities and possibilities of life. And yet in spite of everything, home is still a place where we have considerable scope, at least in principle, for leading our personal lives according to free choices that we make.

Negotiating home life

An idea indelibly associated with politics is that it concerns who has control over something, usually some territory, resource, means of producing or acquiring something, and so on. Although most of us have been taught to assume that a political process entails settlement of competing claims or resolution of conflicting, even mutually hostile, interests, clearly this is not always the case—nor, ideally, does a political process need to take this form. For especially within a smaller circle of people, like a family, a group of roommates, or a couple, mutual understanding and respect can prevail. A decision to share things equally and fairly is therefore as genuine an outcome of a political process as any other. This sort of sharing may involve treating one another identically. But just as likely to eventuate is a give-and-take relationship in which people's differing abilities to contribute to the good of the whole group are recognized, as well as their differing preferences in regard to what they receive in return.

And so the management of home space often turns out to resemble a compact or contract (e.g. 'I'll cook if you'll clean'; 'I'll look after my younger brothers and sisters one night a week if you'll raise my allowance'; 'I'll take out the garbage and manage the accounts in exchange for having the biggest bedroom'). The kind of living situation envisioned here may be guided and sustained by an explicitly formulated set of rules, which may be agreed upon by the various parties, or may be purely ad hoc.

Changing roles

'A woman's place is in the home.' This well-worn saying might make us wince, as it grates against today's quest for sexual equality and freedom of self-determination. It also presupposes a notion of home that is claustrophobic, one-sided, and demeaning to females.

The same applies to the proverb, 'Men build houses; women build homes'. These utterances, once considered venerable pieces of folk wisdom, are now just quaint and offensive relics from the past. What this tells us is that in significant ways, people now expect from home more than they previously have—or at least many people do.

The image of a home as typically occupied by a white, nuclear, middle-class family, in which the father is the dedicated breadwinner, the mother the inexhaustible, yet tidy housewife and ready romantic partner, and the residence filled with desirable furnishings and appliances, has been very influential in recent Western history. Other images previously shaped for centuries (and continue to shape) the way people think and act. All such norms contain often unnoticed assumptions about race, economic status, division of labour, the forms of self-fulfilment that are natural or appropriate for each sex, the requirements for functional efficiency of a home, and so forth. They may also exhibit a high degree of illusion (Box 6).

Box 6 Thoughts about home are entangled in an ideology and economy of desire-fulfilment

Working-class women have not found a home in middle-class America. Not really. Recalling the struggle against the dirt and filth of poverty, they try to make of their small and modest homes, safe, clean places.... They are encouraged to experience the good life vicariously through soap operas, supermarket tabloids, and TV sitcoms.... Working-class women are called on to do the work more privileged men and women do not want to do. They clean; they cook; they care for children.... They labor in factories and mills.

Working-class women do not have optional safety valves; they cannot 'get away' by hopping on a plane or going on a buying spree to relieve depression and monotony.... They dream of

> home ownership because a house provides one of the few places
> where they might have some control over their own lives.
>
> (Janet Zandy, 'Introduction', in *Calling Home: Working-Class Women's Writings—An Anthology*, pp. 1–2, 5–6)

Some argue that media representations of home life influence citizens to internalize and act in accordance with them, which in turn reinforces the values and status quo depicted. This then furthers the interests of those with political and economic power over us (leaders or rulers; producers of consumer goods; perhaps even the military). We would probably all agree that it is one thing to make the choices we do in full recognition of their overall significance, and another to make them without such recognition. But perhaps the truth of what we do lies somewhere in between.

In Figure 7, an illustration from a 1957 issue of *John Bull*, a popular British magazine, we see depicted the kind of family standardized by the media of the time in Great Britain and America as typical or ideal home occupants. However accurate this portrayal may be, historical circumstances and demographic shifts on both sides of the Atlantic have rendered the image an obsolete and self-satirizing caricature. Some experience nostalgia for this time period, but for most people, including those who lived through it, the gender role models projected here are restricted and stultifying.

The illustration immediately tells us several things. The husband and wife spend their days in different spheres; his is external to the house and hers mostly internal to it, except when duties like food shopping and tending to children's needs require otherwise. (We do not, by the way, have to ask whether this couple is married, for that is a given of the era.) Now look more closely at a few details. He is dressed in the suit/tie/overcoat/hat style of the white-collar working world and, with his slicked-down hair, he is

7. Idealized domestic scene of a 1950s British family.

primed to achieve success there. He may have just returned from a business trip, as the children seem to be tearing into a bag he's brought, containing gifts for them. In any event, he brings news from the serious outside world, as symbolized by the newspaper under his arm. In contrast, she is dressed in a neutral-coloured, below-knee dress, and is wearing impossibly high-heeled shoes.

She bends slightly over the stovetop, where dinner appears to be about ready, perfectly timed for his arrival. The kitchen is spotless and she shows suitable relaxed joy at seeing him. Everything is in place: her hair recently tended to, her makeup fresh, her apron defining her homemaker role, and the children scrubbed and well-dressed. We expect that he will want to freshen up briefly and perhaps sit down for a drink before eating, and that she will accommodate this desire by keeping the food warm and joining him for a few minutes. After dinner, he will no doubt sit down with his pipe and slippers, and read the newspaper or watch some TV with the family before she gets the children ready for bed and cleans up. He may even wipe the dishes dry as she washes them, or read to the children.

Portrayals like this, which carry so much baggage, by no means tell the whole story of how family life was in a particular time and place. But they did (and do) reinforce stereotypes people feel pressured to consciously or unconsciously live up to. If they manage to conform, then they can feel good about themselves; and if they don't, they may experience guilt and insecurity. The power of the media, then as now, is to present models of being and behaviour that a person learns to use as a measure of him- or herself. Thus, images of daily life not only purport to represent statistical norms, but also become aspirational norms. Yet it is important to realize that these role models are imaginary constructs, projecting social approval more than truth. It may be observed too that a very circumscribed role for one gender dictates the same for the other. The nine-to-five desk job of the sole breadwinner, toadying to his boss, and competing for advancement with his co-workers, incurs significant lifestyle sacrifices, as the man misses out on many facets of his children's development, and on knowing the personality and capabilities of his spouse at a deeper level.

Home is the place where all of these dynamics intersect, which is what historically makes it a problematic space, shaped as it is from both inside and outside by tradition, convention, and the currents of change. Given all this, it's no wonder that feminists from the 19th century to the present have proposed the redesign of domestic space, featuring shared workspaces, childcare, and more, in order to free women from isolating, daily chores performed in the home.

Domestic abuse and misery

Reconciliation of interests and harmonious group living are challenging projects. Some people can handle them and others, for various reasons, cannot. Unlike the negotiated, mutually satisfactory arrangements described earlier, there is also the all-too-common situation in which equality and fairness do not prevail at home. This leads to the consequence that one or more members of the household feel insecure, alienated, threatened, or less than a person in some way because of the degraded quality of the home environment—and possibly also fear being victims of overt violence. Most sexual and other violent assaults are against females, and occur at home. Although many incidents go unreported, findings by the UN show that an average of 35 per cent of females worldwide have experienced them. A substantial number of males too are victims of domestic violence. Furthermore, a high proportion of murders are committed in the home by someone known to the victim. Sexual, child, and spousal abuse (whether physical, psychological, or both) often provide reasons for leaving home and even becoming homeless (Box 7).

'Home sweet home—but is it so sweet, or has it been so sweet?' asks philosopher Agnes Heller. 'The familiar gesture can be the hand raised to beat.... Home is where we were weeping, but no one listened, where we were hungry and cold. Home was the small circle one could not break through, the childhood that seemed endless, the tunnel without exit.' She speaks here on behalf of many who were unable to escape intolerable living situations, and may have buried and continue to bury their fears, discouragements, and injuries under years of silence. (Some adults who have grown up in

> **Box 7 'Kayla', having left a violent and neglectful parental home and now a mother in her mid-teens, has to flee her second home to escape an abusive partner**
>
> We were actually living in a caravan park and we were getting evicted and I thought, 'Here's my chance to leave him', because I was getting so hurt and my daughter was in the middle of everything. I actually moved into a youth refuge, and he couldn't be there. I had our daughter and he was coming round every day and all of a sudden I just said, 'Look, it's over. Go away, I don't want you anymore'. He hounded me for quite a few months until he got locked up.
>
> (Interview with 'Kayla', in *Moving Out, Moving On: Young People's Pathways In and Through Homelessness*, p. 82)

orphanages point out that life there, though limited in certain ways, was far better than in the home they left behind.)

Much attention has been directed in recent times to exploitation—in particular, forms of gender inequality. These do not necessarily entail sexual abuse, and may have more to do with sex-role stereotyping, such as men's expectations of women's subservience and compliance, and women's lack of economic and personal independence. Sexual inequality also concerns assumed areas of male and female responsibility: the real or perceived split between public and private life; monetarily valued (salaried) work vs. non-remunerated work (housekeeping and childcare); recognition and non-recognition of achievement; aspirations realized and unrealized; and available opportunities for shaping one's self-image, self-esteem, and sense of self-worth.

Colonization

There are larger dimensions of politics relating to homelands and home occupancy as well. One concerns the displacement and dispossession of native peoples. Throughout history, invasions have led to the expansion of empires, the subjugation and assimilation of peoples, and sometimes their extermination or decimation. The plundering and destruction of homes and communities was and still is a regular cause of population dispersals and forced migrations. Many of today's nations are the result of colonization that started during the busiest period of exploration and discovery, the early 15th to 17th centuries. And some are the outcome of later colonial expansions. On a micro-scale, the process that has enabled settlements to claim certain lands and then become well-established cities illustrates the invisible but not wholly forgotten political history of contemporary home emplacement. Geographer Nicholas Blomley points out, for instance, that Vancouver was 'superimposed upon a network of ancient native villages, resource sites, and symbolic landscapes'. The same may be said of many other urban areas—and although the results of history cannot be undone, many would urge that this understanding should be made familiar to those who experience the benefits of dwelling in a place, in order that they might experience significant links with the past and show gratitude in some manner. In Australia, for instance, conferences and other events are routinely opened with an acknowledgement of the 'traditional owners of the land' on which the gathering is taking place. The question 'Who really belongs in this place that we live in today?' is one that most people would perhaps deny as valid—but others would at least feel some uneasiness in confronting it and find it a stimulus to reflection.

Traditional indigenous societies had a different conception of land and place, as Chapter 2 revealed. A large part of the history of these peoples over the past few centuries has been the imposition on them of the 'propertied' conception of land and place, mainly by British, European, and American explorers, conquistadors, settlers, and entrepreneurs. For native peoples in various places, the environments they had occupied for vast periods of time were sacred and beyond value—shared domains that defined them as

the cultures they were. *Their environments were home to them.*
Anthropologist Hugh Brody argues that hunter-gatherer societies
did not seek to transform the surrounding land they inhabited but
to live according to its patterns and rhythms, finding everything
they needed within it, respecting it as an 'Eden' in the here and
now. Other anthropologists, for example Riane Eisler and
Marja Gimbutas, go even further, documenting an account
of European prehistoric civilization that shows it to have
been goddess-worshipping, matriarchal, egalitarian, and
Earth-protecting. These practices and principles were displaced
several millennia BCE, yielding to those of the patriarchal societies
we find in control today. The foreign invaders who plundered and
eventually confiscated customary territories of indigenous peoples
showed little or no understanding of or respect for the ideas such
cultures embodied, and supplanted them as quickly as possible
with their own, while also indoctrinating the people they
conquered with alien religious beliefs.

When traditional societies lose their autonomy and ability to
range over their lands, they also suffer a devastating blow to their
cultural identities and sense of belonging to a particular home
place. It is nearly impossible for outsiders to gauge the extent of
this harm and how profoundly it can disorient the psyche, but the
results are still seen today in many locations around the world.
And even if the political will existed to support remedial measures
or reparations, what might be appropriate and beneficial at this
stage of history is difficult to determine. However, these issues
continue to be pressing today. Ingetje Tadros, a photojournalist,
spent several months in a remote Western Australian Aboriginal
community—one of many that face the prospect of being
defunded and closed down by the state government as 'unviable'.
Her observation is that 'Taking Country away from people is like
committing spiritual genocide.' In Canada, Australia, and the US,
'stolen generations' of native children know what this feels like, as
they were forcibly removed from their families, sent to residential
schools, and forbidden to speak their languages or ever see their

parents and communities. In addition, tens of thousands of poor and orphaned British children were sent from their country to the US, Canada, Australia, New Zealand, and South Africa from the 17th to the 20th centuries. Many of these exiled children, like the stolen generations, were subjected to physical and sexual abuse. Their sorrow over lost homes or having no home is profound and lasts a lifetime.

The phenomenon of place or territory that is both cognitively constructed and emotionally framed as home meets us at every turn. Another example concerns the Xhosa people, originally from the Eastern Cape region of South Africa. Like many other black South Africans, the Xhosa have left their homelands in great numbers looking for work, first in the diamond fields opened in the 19th century and later in Cape Town. Over the past three decades, a massive urban influx has occurred, creating Khayelitsha township: 'an enormous sea of shacks and shanties, as densely packed as a medieval city'. But those who live in this township—including generations who have never even visited where the Xhosa came from—are completely committed to being buried 'back home' in the Eastern Cape, and a busy funeral transport industry caters to their wishes.

Fighting for the homeland

Robert Ginsberg suggests that 'Our homeland is our childhood home writ large. It is the largest identifiable realm in which we imagine that we would feel at home and which we feel obligated to protect against foreigners.' The idea of homeland is invoked especially strongly whenever a perceived or imagined external threat appears to require the creation of symbolic and emotional associations that will promote national unity and restore a sense of safety and dominion over territory held dear. This process of forging a connection between homeland and home—almost always aided by propaganda—permits patriotism and one-dimensional thinking to come to the fore ('You're either for us or against us'). People's energies and dedication can then be marshalled by political authorities to meet whatever challenge it is that they've defined for their citizens. Examples are numerous, but the self-declared need, under the Third Reich, to redefine and extend the German homeland, and the obsessive preoccupation with homeland security in various countries today are two that stand out very clearly.

The idea of a homeland is not a bad thing in itself, but when it is used as a fictive device for manipulating the public will, negative impacts are likely to result. A paranoid siege mentality develops; feebly articulated national values are declared as obligatory; the multicultural society that welcomes immigrants becomes in jeopardy as xenophobia manifests itself, for example in public assaults on visible minorities and the vandalizing of their places of worship; heightened airport security becomes a way of life; declarations of war are made on vaguely defined entities, such as 'terror'; and civil rights are abrogated. We are all impoverished by this appropriation of home for political and ideological ends.

Chapter 7
Homelessness and uprootedness

General considerations about homelessness

No discussion of home can be complete without taking account of homelessness, for two reasons. First, those who are lucky enough to have a place to call home owe it to those who aren't so lucky to empathetically understand *their* situation. Second, the absence of home helps us better appreciate the significance of home. Confronting the word 'homeless' conjures up the image of urban street people who are doing it rough, seeking handouts from passersby, and sleeping wherever they can. People who have been left behind and left without can be found everywhere. Homelessness has historically worsened in times of general economic hardship. But the problem of homelessness in the world today is much more profound than one might realize at first.

The categories of homelessness (which are not necessarily mutually exclusive) include: those who chronically have no home; those who no longer have a place to call home because of reduced circumstances; migrants who have had more than one place to call home, but confront issues of who they are and where they truly belong; and those who are spiritually homeless. In this chapter, we look at each of these groups in turn.

Destitution

Homelessness is neither an invention of modern social scientists nor something that just came into existence with industrialization, capitalism, or any other transformative event of recent centuries. Exiles, debtors, vagrants, fugitives, refugees, pilgrims, wanderers: people described (and often self-described) in these ways have been part of human life and culture for a very long time. And scholars have shown that homelessness was a regular feature of the medieval and Renaissance eras both in England and Europe and in countries as distant from each other as Peru and Iceland.

How best to define homelessness is much debated and arguably a matter specific to each culture. Many people would probably say that even if they can't define it, they know it when they see it. Homeless street people make others feel uncomfortable. Why? For one thing, they represent what can go seriously wrong in life, and therefore disrupt contentment and peace of mind. Encountering the homeless may arouse concern, and feelings of guilt and confusion over how to be of help and what society should do to fix the problem. Homeless individuals may be perceived as physically threatening—rightly or wrongly. A common response is to not want to know about the homeless: to ignore them altogether or give them a small offering and then move on. Some even blame the homeless themselves for their plight. But as Tony Clark, who runs the charity Swags for Homeless in Melbourne, observes, 'Nobody wanted to be homeless. Nobody thought, "Hey, when I grow up I'm going to be homeless"'. The newspaper article summarizing Clark's views continues:

> Every vagrant once had a mother and father—a different set of circumstances—and fell on hard times.... For example, you may lose your job and, unable to pay rent, move into a car. 'Things spiral out of control'.

This account receives emphasis from recent news that soaring property prices in the city of Auckland have forced hundreds of families to live in cars, garages, and other makeshift accommodations.

Homelessness is a human plight of serious proportions. The destabilized lives of street people are always at risk owing to health and safety concerns. Genuine shelter, privacy, and a sense of community are temporary and elusive. The homeless comprise not only adults of all ages, but also adolescents and families with children—generally women without partners and with dependants. A majority of homeless persons have backgrounds of extreme poverty, drug or alcohol abuse, or mental illness. In addition, homelessness seriously degrades people's psychological well-being. Writer-comedian Mandy Nolan focuses on this issue when she asks, 'How does a person maintain a sense of who they are and why they are important when they are sleeping on a park bench?' Philosopher Patricia Anne Murphy, who has worked with the homeless for many years, similarly observes that to be homeless 'is to be, at least experientially, diminished in personhood.... This diminishment bleeds into the social and psychological fabric of life.... [It] jeopardizes the development of systems of meaning that are central for the identity of persons.' These meaning-frameworks include things like having a sense of purpose, agency, and worthwhile achievement (for example, being able to set and realize goals or participate in public life in some way), receiving praise and other forms of affirmation and approval from others, and having a place of belonging and safety. As we have seen, such deeper needs are closely allied with the positive meanings of home.

Homeless people's insecure economy revolves around small-scale activities, both legal and illegal, such as panhandling, collecting recyclable items, selling homemade goods, doing odd jobs, petty crime, occasional gifts received from family or friends, and income from miscellaneous sources. Some also resort to work in the various sex trades.

A new kind of effort to reduce homelessness and its social costs known as 'housing first' is being tried in the US and Canada—with positive results. In this scheme, public housing is provided in the belief that what caused an individual's homelessness is better dealt with once he or she has a home and a new vantage-point from which to view and change life circumstances. Following this model, New Orleans has recently become the first US city to get all homeless veterans off the street.

Elsewhere in the world, homelessness has a somewhat different profile. Urban development and planning specialists Susanne Speak and Graham Tipple point out that in poorer countries it is mainly a function of chronic housing shortages, which result in 'massive informal [housing] development and squatting'. 'Indeed,' they rather astonishingly claim, 'most of the world's population would be homeless if judged by the standards of the developed nations'. It's this sort of generalization that leads sociologist Sophie Watson to argue that since homelessness is often confused with houselessness, it has an 'ambiguous nature' and hence, the entire contested notion 'needs to be reconstructed if not abandoned'.

Homelessness as a global concern

Homelessness is not just a problem besetting relatively small groups of unfortunate individuals, however, it exists in a much larger arena. As the United Nations High Commission for Refugees (UNHCR) has recently reported, sixty million people have been displaced globally by war, conflict, and persecution. Of these, 19.5 million are refugees (more than half of them children), 38.2 million are internally displaced (those who have fled their homes, but not crossed an international border), and 1.8 million are asylum seekers. Gillian Triggs, distinguished president of the Australian Human Rights Commission, succinctly observes that 'The movement of people internationally is absolutely unprecedented.' Many experts believe the situation will get even worse. The UNHCR displacement total just cited represents one person out of every 122 on the planet; and if these sixty million persons made up one nation, it would be the world's twenty-fourth largest.

We live in a time when many people are literally fleeing for their lives. Many present themselves as legal immigrants in order to relocate, but others—increasingly, desperately, and determinedly—are negotiating their way through unknown territory and around barriers to safety, or taking to the rough seas in rickety, overcrowded, dangerous vessels, placing themselves at the mercy of the elements and profiteering people-smugglers. Overall, hundreds of thousands of refugees and asylum seekers are fleeing terrible circumstances in any way they can, legal or illegal, to any place they can, and they face an uncertain future. Continuing conflicts in Syria, Afghanistan, Iraq, Pakistan, Nigeria, Somalia, Burundi, and Sudan/South Sudan account for some of the largest single-country displacements. Eleven million Syrians—over half of the country's population—have been displaced by civil and factional warfare. Immense numbers are 'roaming from town to town, looking for safety'. Those killed by conflict total 500,000. An estimated 4.8 million are refugees in other countries. These figures starkly highlight a humanitarian crisis of vast proportions. At the time of writing, the war in eastern Ukraine that began in early 2014 has left more than a million and a half people homeless as well. The stateless Rohingya people of Myanmar (Burma) are fleeing by their thousands but finding no country willing to come to their aid. The current world situation is overwhelming recipient countries in Europe as well as Pakistan, Iran, Jordan, Lebanon, Turkey, Tanzania, Kenya, and Ethiopia. Some EU countries have begun deporting refugees. Asylum seekers from Afghanistan, Iraq, Syria, Serbia and Kosovo, Eritrea, and elsewhere are applying in great numbers for entry into countries as widely separated as Sweden, Ecuador, South Africa, and the US. More than eight thousand refugees have died by drowning in the Mediterranean Sea since 2014.

For every instance of displacement, there is a story (or perhaps several) of homelessness—of tragic events, large and small, happening to groups of ordinary citizens who were just trying to exist peacefully, get by, and raise their families; of dwellings, people, and belongings left behind; of individuals' lives torn apart (Box 8).

Dozens of these personal stories can be found on the UNHCR's website.

Natural and human-made disasters create large-scale homelessness as well. A massive explosion of deadly chemicals at a plant in Tianjin, North China, on 12 August 2015 killed well

Box 8 War has created tragedy for the residents of Kobani in Northern Syria

'There are no words coming back to a destroyed city that was your home', said Shamsa Shahinzada, an architect who fled Kobani before Isis arrived and who was our guide to the shattered remains, still off-limits to most of its former inhabitants. 'This was the main square where people crowded every week to ask for freedom', she said, eyes filling with tears as she saw what was left of Kobani's centre. 'This was our friend's home, we used to stay there. Beside there, there was a school—my high school.' . . .

Idriss Nassan, deputy head of the government, added, 'Unfortunately the city is destroyed, but people have memories here and this is our land. We don't want to move everything from here.'

(Emma Graham-Harrison, 'Kobani: Destroyed and Riddled with Unexploded Bombs, but its Residents Dare to Dream of a New Start', *The Guardian*)

over one hundred people, injured several hundred others, and displaced over 6,000. Nepal's 7.8 magnitude earthquake on 25 April 2015 killed 9,000 people, and many thousands more were injured and left homeless. In one district, 95 per cent of homes were destroyed. And, as in many tragedies of this kind, infrastructure was also decimated, making a semblance of normal life difficult even when alternative forms of shelter were made available. The Philippines was hit on 8 November 2013 by one of the most severe cyclones ever recorded anywhere. Typhoon Haiyan (also called Yolanda) claimed more than 6,000 lives, displaced over four million, and destroyed or damaged one million homes. Recovery and rebuilding is ongoing. Pakistan is prone to frequent flooding and, during the August–September 2011 period, hundreds perished in the Sindh floods, 'with 5.3 million people and 1,534,773 homes affected'. Earlier the same year (11 March), a major earthquake and 15-metre tsunami killed 19,000 people and caused a nuclear power station meltdown in Fukushima, Japan. Despite massive clean-up operations, few of the 160,000 forced to abandon the area are willing to return. Haiti suffered a 7.0 magnitude earthquake on 12 January 2010. With the epicentre near Port-au-Prince, 230,000 people were killed and 1.5 million left homeless. Haiti was already one of the world's poorest nations before this event occurred. On 29 August 2005, Hurricane Katrina pounded the iconic US city of New Orleans, causing widespread flooding and damage. The city's population has taken years to recover, and there are abundant stories of personal tragedy and neglect by authorities, from the White House down to the local level. Perhaps the most telling fact about this episode is that 'Many low-income New Orleans evacuees spent several years after the storm in nomadic exile, moving among family members' residences or in search of jobs or housing.' Emotional disturbances, missing school, bullying, and discrimination were often experienced by children from this group. Homelessness on such large scales is socially and politically catastrophic, and especially of course for the individuals directly affected.

The dispossessed

Many events have also created disconnection, loss of direction, and a homeless condition for peoples who least expected it, as the following two examples show. Diego Garcia, an island under British sovereignty, is part of the Chagos Archipelago in the central Indian Ocean. The UK and US decided they wanted a military base located there, and so between 1968 and 1973 the resident population of several thousand was forced to leave by various unpleasant means and taken to Mauritius and the Seychelles. What they left behind was 'abundant fish, a culture of sharing and a peaceful way of life that lasted generations'. Displaced Chagossians have fared poorly in other lands, and have experienced a sense of deep loss over their exile. The military installation continues to operate, and an international campaign to support repatriation is ongoing.

Brazil, a rising world economic power, is looking to produce more and cheaper energy, while meeting its targets to help reduce global warming. Current government policy favours the pursuit of massive hydroelectric projects, the latest of which is the 5-kilometre-long Belo Monte dam across the Xingu River in Amazonia. It will be the world's fourth largest. As in the case of dams in many other countries, sizeable groups of people will lose their homes and/or homelands. Indigenous tribes have fought in vain to prevent their ancestral lands—richly endowed rain forests—from being flooded, and their way of life from being destroyed. The dam, now mired in legal challenges, failed to be completed in time for the 2016 Brazil-hosted Olympics as planned, and will likely not be finished before 2019.

These stories of homelessness and loss, caused by forced relocation that is not the result of war and violence (at least in the conventional sense), could be multiplied endlessly. As is the case with other instances of international migration covered in this

8. **Cambodian protesters in Phnom Penh take a stand against home evictions for new private developments.**

chapter, these two stories could also be examined under the heading of 'the politics of home' applied in a wider sense (see Chapter 6). The fact is that many people in the world do not have a great deal of say in regard to keeping their homes, and face a stark existence whether they end up losing them to a bank that forecloses on a mortgage or as a result of larger events that negate their will (see Figure 8).

International migrants

Migration and settlement have been the engines of human life since its earliest days. In the present moment, the flow of people taking up residence in other countries keeps setting new records. As reported by the United Nations, the latest figures show an annual total of 232 million international migrants, with a yearly increase of 1.6 per cent. This total falls between the populations of Brazil and Indonesia, which rank fifth and fourth, respectively, among the world's most populous nations.

In the overall picture, international migrants are of two kinds: migrants by choice and by necessity, though the boundary line between them is often somewhat blurred. A 'diaspora', for instance, is historically considered to be an involuntarily scattered or dispersed (sometimes persecuted and disenfranchised) ethnic or religious group. But in more modern terms, as international migration specialist Khalid Koser notes, it may just be 'a large group of people with a similar heritage or homeland who have since moved out to places all over the world'. While many migrants readily adjust to previously 'foreign' lands and come to feel comfortable in the community of which they are part (Box 9), others face greater difficulty in meeting the challenges of relocation.

Those having adequate means, freedom, and motivation visit where they came from one or more times. It is not uncommon for

Box 9 An immigrant speaks about her sense of belonging

Giselle Cohen, 89 years old, has lived in Australia for seventy-seven years since immigrating from Germany in 1938 at age 13. On 24 January 2015, Australia Day, she remarked in an interview that: 'When we first landed here...it was a very hot day, asphalt melting under foot, and I thought where the hell are we?...[A few years later] I travelled back to Europe and revisited Germany but I was never so happy as when I came back here because I felt this was home. I felt the camaraderie, I felt at ease.... The opportunities we all have...are enormous, and life here is generally enviable to many other nations.

For me, Australia has become home. The essence of Australia is in me. I [am]...happy to be part of a country that has been so generous. We should always feel a sense of celebration.'

(Giselle Cohen, interview, 'Diverse Journeys', pp. 16–17)

them to maintain and nurture ties with friends and family 'back home' (with quite a number sending money to relatives on a regular basis), to become bilingual or multilingual, and to hold more than one passport. These people belong to what Koser calls a 'transnational community', within which people 'are beginning to escape the confines of political definitions such as immigrant or citizen'.

The challenge migrants generally face is to find a way of being that is both a commitment to a fresh start and a way of still respecting and embodying older allegiances—somehow merging the old and new identities. Filmmaker Gurinder Chadha (*Bend It Like Beckham*), born in Kenya of Indian parents, and raised and now living in London, provides an interesting example of this process. During a trip to discover her Indian roots for the television programme *Who Do You Think You Are?*, she remarks: 'I have no concept of an ancestral home, or in fact a homeland....Whilst [India] is still not home...this feels really good, to be standing on the soil of where I know that my ancestors came from over four thousand years ago.' More tales of this sort form the content of the ABC-TV (Australia) programme *Home Delivery*, hosted by Julia Zamiro.

For others, there is a less happy story to tell. Some migrants will never see their land of origin again, even though they might dearly wish to. A great deal of pain may be felt by those who think of themselves as having left a traditional homeland behind, perhaps permanently, and who long for a reunion with this place of spiritual, geopolitical, or environmental origin, a place where the person has either formed or is yearning to form a sense of self-understanding. Some people think of a place as home because of a familial connection, even though they may have never been there. If 'home is where the heart is', then a *de facto* home (where one is actually living) may not equate to one's emotional home; it perhaps lies elsewhere and is in the realm of things beyond recovery (Box 10).

Box 10 The immigrant's dilemma is one of identity

The migrant background—the double one, Lebanese and English—gave me, I think, a particular sense of how accidental, how contingent the facts of a life may be. For many migrants who came to Australia, as my mother did, in late childhood, when their lives had already begun to assume an expected shape, translation to the new place was never quite complete; the old one continued in a ghostly way as an alternative life unlived, a promise broken.

For all its being daily and real, life in the new place had an accidental or provisional quality. I sensed this quite strongly in my mother and felt it again later in others. Closely related to this was the accidental quality of what I felt *I* was.

(David Malouf, 'My multicultural life', pp. 30–1)

A variety of means, including membership in associations and the use of social media, help many migrants connect with compatriots also residing within their new country, in a bid to create meaningful relationships, forge a sense of place, and facilitate participation in public and civic life. But it seems clear that for all migrants, gaining a new sense of belonging and being at home is a complex, ongoing balancing act. Aboriginal Australian lawyer and land rights activist Noel Pearson puts forward the idea that migrants have 'layered identities', embracing both 'individuality and commonality'. People, places, language, clothing, customs, food, religion, music, history, material goods, special souvenirs and mementos, photographs, and other symbolic and personal associations all enter into the equation, yielding different resolutions to the problems of 'fitting in'. In Santiago, Chile, for example, the largest Palestinian community outside of the Middle East mixes at its own café; at the local playing field to cheer on its own professional soccer team; and at a neighbourhood club, which boasts a swimming pool, parks, and gardens. For some, a 'home away from home' makes sense—just as a 'home from home' does for those who are not themselves migrants, but are used to a routine of spending significant portions of their lives living in more than one place.

Although it is difficult to generalize, it seems likely that migrants by necessity might suffer the loss of place in a more acute fashion, but this does not serve as a reliable indicator that they would take longer than migrants by choice to come to terms with residing in a new and unfamiliar country. Some migrants will always yearn for what they have left behind, the urge to go back home being very strong. 'My biggest wish in life is that we return to our country and stay there forever,' says Eqleema, an 11-year-old Afghan female refugee living in Pakistan. For others, life is better elsewhere. Clarisse, a 15-year-old girl from the Democratic Republic of Congo—a refugee settled in Phoenix, US—reports, 'we've made lots of new friends…my sister and I want to stay here forever'. In any event, not all migrants are destined to stay and to never return to their place of origin. As an interesting aside to this discussion, some migrants by choice who later return to where they came from seem to forfeit happiness at both ends of their journey. Anthropologist Daniel Miller reports, for instance, that Jamaicans who had moved to England and been unhappy there found, on going back to Jamaica, that they still did not feel at home, were not welcome, and had become somewhat lost souls.

Modern culture unmoored

Simone Weil, French thinker, essayist, mystic, and political activist, once wrote that 'To be rooted is perhaps the most important and least recognized need of the human soul.' Hungarian philosopher and critic Geörgy Lukács puts forward the now-familiar idea that in at least some earlier societies, people possessed an integrated sense of wholeness and continuity—of where everything fitted within a larger scheme. Their own lives could therefore be understood as being anchored and possessed of meaning. They were 'at home' not just in the place they inhabited, but also within their own skins and minds. Ancient Greek philosophy and epic poems illustrated this phenomenon, according to Lukács. In contrast, modern novels are characterized by what he provocatively calls 'transcendental homelessness', which is a reflection of the human situation at present, where meaning and groundedness in the world must continuously be sought after and struggled for, rather than being found near at hand. 'Our world has become infinitely large and each of its corners is richer in gifts and dangers than the world of the Greeks, but such wealth cancels out the positive meaning—the totality—upon which their life was based.' Lukács contends that where larger, encompassing certainties no longer guide us and everything is questionable and questioned, the task of literature is to come to terms with the loss of totality that is so widely experienced, and to achieve some form of closure by creating new mental spaces where people can recover a sense of home.

In their important 1970s study *The Homeless Mind*, sociologists Peter L. Berger, Brigitte Berger, and Hansfried Kellner explain that 'To be human means to live in a world—that is, to live in a reality that is ordered and that gives sense to the business of living.' But, they continue, *'modern man has suffered from a deepening condition of "homelessness"'*. A number of factors contribute to the evolution of this condition, the most weighty of which, in their view, is the decline of religion: 'Modern society has threatened the plausibility of religious theodicies [attempts to reconcile evil with the goodness and justice of the universe], but it has not removed the experiences that call for them.' And well before the 'selfie' age, Berger, Berger, and Kellner cite the retreat into the private sphere of individualism as 'Modern society's "solution" to these discontents'.

American radical culture critic and activist Susan Sontag also detected the presence of homelessness as a dominant theme and message in contemporary literature and the arts generally. In a 1961 essay, she argued that

> Most serious thought in our time struggles with the feeling of homelessness. The felt unreliability of human experience brought about by the inhuman acceleration of historical change has led every sensitive modern mind to the recording of some kind of nausea, of intellectual vertigo.

A raft of cultural figures fit in here, such as Jean-Paul Sartre, author of the novel *Nausea*; Albert Camus, whose enduring character is 'the outsider'; Samuel Beckett, who offered 'waiting' as a metaphor for the human condition (as in *Waiting for Godot*); and Martin Heidegger, whose *Letter on Humanism* describes how humanity has lost its way in the contemporary world. These sorts of figures strongly express what is often called the temper of the time, the collective consciousness of an era.

But is it truly our era? This may well be debated, and some might dismiss the cultural tendencies singled out for attention here as expressions of the world-weariness, alienation, melancholy, and disillusionment fostered by the Industrial Revolution, the rise of totalitarianism, two World Wars, and the Great Depression. This is simplistic, however, for three reasons. The first is that characterizing our existential predicament as one of homelessness is not new. In the 17th century, Blaise Pascal, French philosopher, mathematician, early game theorist, and maverick defender of the Christian faith, wrote in his *Pensées* (*Meditations*) that humans cling to an untethered existence in the enormity of a universe they cannot comprehend. But it's not just that knowledge of our origin, purpose, and ultimate destiny escapes us, living itself discloses our state of being as vagabonds in the cosmos. Second, the cataclysmic world events listed earlier have had repercussions that we very much live with today. And the third point is that events subsequent to these—the Cold War, Vietnam War, wars in the

Middle East, globalization, climate change, the Global Financial Crisis, and the rise of terrorism and refugeeism—are monumentally destabilizing and are disorienting contemporary life pretty nearly everywhere.

There are numerous ways in which this somewhat abstract discussion connects with everyday life, for example in relation to the experience of being black in America. J.C. Faulk, an African-American community organizer in Baltimore, sums it up this way:

> Black people have been living in this culture for centuries and we're afraid of the system that's supposed to be protecting us. It's like we're in a place that is home on some levels or another, but it never feels like home; it always feels like you're someplace you're not supposed to be.

This is a real, lived condition for many people of colour.

Whether those who speak of homelessness as the miasma of modern and/or postmodern life have any real solutions to offer to the crisis of the soul they posit is unclear; they seldom take on the gritty task of defining what sort of cultural and/or individual project it might be to recover a larger sense of home (which we will consider in Chapter 8). Nevertheless, to speak of homelessness in the broad sense discussed earlier has struck many as an illuminating way of identifying the manner in which contemporary cultures seem to be unravelling. Yet we do not have to subscribe to any 'ism' or school of thought in order to appreciate that much of present-day life is characterized by fragmentation of interests, cynicism, a sense of exile, alienation and disillusionment, lack of faith in authorities (people, institutions, belief systems), plus the search for holistic approaches that make sense of our outward experience and our inner thoughts and feelings.

An afterthought

Unless we can trace our lineage to the original humans and find that we live where they lived, we are all international migrants. Furthermore, we are all wanderers. We symbolically carry our homes on our backs, like turtles, snails, and crustaceans—for the meanings and associations of home are always with us and affect our orientation in space and time, and how we negotiate our way through the world. As we have also seen, there are numerous varieties of homelessness, and therefore having a home is something never to be taken for granted.

Chapter 8
The future of home

Through a glass darkly

Thinking about the future is unavoidable. For practical reasons, individuals, groups, and societies need to make plans, and this entails looking ahead. And as creative and curious beings, the imagined future is where we test out our ideas and projects. Futurology is risky, however. Certain trends that will shape things to come are already visible and even obvious, which leads some to speak of 'the foreseeable future'. But if we are honest with ourselves, the longer term future is no more foreseeable than the past is changeable. On the positive side, the sky's the limit so far as the future is concerned. There are indefinitely numerous new ideas and technologies—many as yet unknown or barely discernible—that might develop and improve the quality of life *if* humans have the good sense to protect their planet's health, learn to live in peace with one another, and choose to share resources and opportunities more equitably. Only in this way will there be a future at all and one that is worth living in, unlike the apocalyptic versions presented by today's film and fiction.

Some constants

When in human evolutionary history did home begin; when did the first homes come into being? This question is unanswerable with any degree of certainty, both because of the limitations of archaeological evidence and also because of the diversity of opinion on how 'home' should be defined. The assumption made in this book is that homes have existed as long as people have lived together, in whatever cultural configurations they have developed (see Chapter 3). It is of course a very long historical journey from home viewed as a special space, landscape, and ecosystem to designated, circumscribed dwellings; and, along a different line of development, from the most undifferentiated homes, in which everything occurs within communal space, to so-called 'modern' homes, in which individuals have their own personal space. Philosopher Frederick Olafson maintains that it has also been a very long journey to the age of individuality itself:

> It would not, I think, be an exaggeration to say that for the first time in human history, large numbers of human beings have come to think of themselves as autonomous moral agents, capable of raising and resolving for themselves all questions about what they are to do.

The basis for this claim is that in earlier centuries, even millennia, the struggle for existence, as well as social and economic restrictions, prevented a high degree of self-reflection and personal freedom from emerging on a wide scale. And today still, many forces conspire to undermine individuality and its expression in the public sphere, and in many places human dignity and personal inviolability are constantly under threat and attack.

To be a private self or distinct individual—a centre of attention for its own sake—requires private space in which to grow and take stock of the world. But this is only part of what makes us human. People will always need to achieve a sense of self-identity, of belonging in and to the world, and of social and cultural membership. Individual and group dynamics are interdependent. For settled cultures, thoughts about home have traditionally provided people with a firm sense of who they were and where they fit in, and why. Displaced or dispersed cultures yearn for home because this firm sense has been disrupted and essential connections that define them have been severed. We can't just define ourselves, by ourselves, in an asocial vacuum.

Anthropologist and creative writer Michael Jackson has spent decades studying the ways in which people in various parts of the world live and establish themselves somewhere that is meaningful to them. Based on a wide range of evidence and immersion in the study of cultures past and present, Jackson states that the central question guiding his research is 'how...people transform givenness into choice so that the world into which they are thrown becomes a world they can call their own'. He continues: 'This existential project is, I believe, a universal human imperative....We often say that we feel at home in the world when what we do has some effect and what we say carries some weight....In this sense, at-homeness suggests an elusive balance which people try to strike between being acted upon and acting, between acquiescing in the given and choosing their own fate.' We have been looking at home as a concept that is universal and essential for grounding ourselves in the world. But home also forms a bridge to something even deeper: finding an anchor in existence. And those daily activities of connection that express the best of our humanity—community development and involvement, peaceful coexistence with one other and with other species, sustainability practices, understanding the rhythms of whatever place we're in—help to maintain this anchor. What Jackson adds to the mix is the important insight that being at home signifies a quest for empowerment, for feeling efficacious and responsible for ourselves within the world to a realistic and satisfying extent.

This illuminates some of the problems we have examined in Chapters 6 and 7. There is little to romanticize or wax nostalgic about concerning a home place one has left behind because of its oppressiveness or because of the routine, impoverished, spirit-numbing life one was forced to lead there. It is just as true today as it was in the past that people will seek an escape from their homebound situation in order, they hope, to better their lot someplace else, and are often able to recognize instantly when they have succeeded. It is an innate human impulse to seek to dwell where self-affirmation, attachment, and belonging come alive. And if you already are in such a place, it is one of the greatest sacrifices to leave it behind. No one who has seen the 1982 movie *E.T.: The Extra-Terrestrial* can possibly forget the poignant scene where the eponymous alien wistfully wails 'Home!' while pointing towards outer space. That cleverly drove home the point about home: that it is an inescapable reference point for individual orientation in existence. It follows that we can expect homes—whatever their type—to exist and continue serving the same needs in the future as they have always done (Box 11).

Box 11 How things look, when all is said and done: some central ideas about home

Positive/aspirational concepts of home

The place where I happen to live now or once did—or both.

The place from which I originate (homeland).

The place where I discover who I am, have my strongest emotional ties, and am anchored by memories essential to my life-narrative.

The place where my ethnic, national, religious identity is most strongly affirmed and reinforced.

The place where I have my spiritual, ancestral, or other special roots (my country, where I grew up).

The place where I belong, feel safe, and am valued.

Home as a physical place or location

Geographical territory, unit, sub-unit.

Specific piece of land or environment/habitat.

My specific abode or dwelling unit and its material environment.

My planned or ideal abode/dwelling and its material environment.

Community, neighbourhood.

Built dwelling, on land that is privately owned, communally owned, government owned, rented/leased, or just occupied.

General functions of home

Durable or habitual shelter.

Housing for family, intimates, casual acquaintances.

Venue for relationship-formation and nurturing.

Satisfying material environment.

Domain of privacy.

Provision of stability and rejuvenation to actively face the world.

Living in a world of rapid change

There is no denying that change is a hallmark of our age, and that the rate of change is increasing. Many towns and communities around the world struggle to survive and remain viable centres of habitation. In Portugal and Spain, falling birth rates and economic hardship are decimating rural areas, and the same trends are taking over in other European countries. According to one report, 'As young people depart, they leave villages of empty houses and shuttered shops, of closed schools and cafés.... Fields carefully tended for centuries are left uncultivated and overgrown. Farms and outbuildings crumble from neglect.' Large cities around the world groan under the pressure to meet the requirements, expectations, and desires of rapidly expanding populations, often in the absence of much planning or ethical and legal frameworks to guide transition into the future. Internet commerce, increasing amounts of travel, commuting to jobs in other locations, and the relocation of old and the influx of new residents are forces that both invigorate and deplete places where people live. Yet the ingrained human drive to achieve affinity with their surroundings and self-fulfilment nevertheless continues to express itself in identification with a particular location. This drive asserts itself in widely differing circumstances and finds many outlets for materialization.

Early North American pioneers and migrating groups in many regions of the world struggled to carve out a niche for themselves in often excruciatingly inhospitable environments—to create outposts of hope and personal freedom where they could flourish and consolidate their identities. These same motivations and energies are apparent even in the vast urban centres of today. Cities like Mumbai (formerly Bombay), Kinshasa, Manila, Mexico City, Jakarta, Ho Chi Minh City (formerly Saigon), Rio de Janeiro, Bangkok, Lagos, and Buenos Aires are often stereotyped as chaotic and seemingly out of control. Large urban settings like these suffer from the blights of overpopulation, poverty, lack of zoning regulations, pollution, high crime rates, corruption, and so on. Many inhabitants grind out the most meagre daily existence, living on the edge of squalid dumpsites, in super-dense ghettos, or as squatters on public land. Moving from the countryside to the city may amount to little more than exchanging one type of toil and struggle for another. Yet life amazingly goes on and exhibits incredible tenacity and resilience. As one commentator observes,

> [S]ome of the oldest cities in the world are located in Africa, Asia and Latin America, which means they have evolved over millennia. Furthermore, what makes the order of the material city in these regions particularly unique is the presence of informal settlements, which are entire neighborhoods and mini-cities built entirely from scratch. They are examples of stunning resourcefulness of those with lowest access to financial and material resources. In that way, even with their myriad problems, they are beautiful testaments to human ingenuity.

9. Hand-made home in a big city.

There is nothing good about extreme poverty; but the point here is that there's a certain quiet dignity that people assert when they create and adorn even the most minimal shelter and living space, making it something to call their own. (See Figure 9.)

In pursuit of stability

Some experts on home characterize it as an entity in constant, even restless transformation. As people change, interact, and major events occur, home evolves accordingly. We could probably also characterize what we think about home as a collection of sometimes contradictory ideas and feelings. Yet paradoxically, and to a significant extent, stability is what home represents. Perhaps this discrepancy can be explained by the fact that at home, one tends to feel more in control of things.

For many reasons, stability has become an elusive quality of life in the present era. The quest for stability may help illuminate some home-making and home-occupying tendencies, such as the inclination to preserve, restore, and renovate older homes, which aims to achieve a kind of wholeness or completeness in one's immediate environment. 'A man's home is his castle.' In terms of today's housing prices, who could judge otherwise? But in a more serious vein, the stresses of modern life do make men *and* women feel that their home is a kind of sanctuary. Stay-at-home types, whom we call 'home bodies' or people who 'keep themselves to themselves', seek the protection of home because they can't deal very well with the outside world, or are strongly introverted, antisocial, or fearful. And there are those who have a besieged-castle mentality and retreat home because they experience their multicultural society-in-flux as a series of threats to all they hold dear. Yet home may nevertheless survive these challenges of meaning as a normative or aspirational idea that persists in exercising its influence over everyone in some fashion.

A series of research studies conducted over the past decade on three continents showed that, contrary to what many might believe or predict, ethnically diverse communities promote tolerance over time rather than the reverse, and positively enrich individuals' awareness of their neighbourhoods. The sense of home as a place of stability and calm is bound to be nourished as well. And so it may happen that those countries that are losing population will be saved from decline and rejuvenated by the new wave of refugees resettling in them.

The quest for stability also surfaces in the desire of older people to remain at home and to maintain (for the rest of their lives, if possible) their independence and connections with familiar and cherished physical surroundings. 'For many old people...the experience of home has taken on new meaning [which] is largely tied to memories and to things', notes psychologist and communications professor Kenneth Doyle. Hence, well-being in old age is nurtured by being able to continue living at home. As surgeon and writer Atul Gawande remarks, 'Home is the one place where your own priorities hold sway. At home, you decide how you spend your time, how you share your space, and how you manage your possessions. Away from home, you don't.'

The wish to die at home, in the presence of loved ones, remains very strong in many individuals. Present trends being what they are, however (at least in Western countries), most people are less likely to realize this ideal than to die in an institutional setting. But given the choice between that and dying alone and lonely, probably most would prefer being looked after by specialized medical staff in a quality treatment facility.

Beyond home?

While home may provide some ingredients that are necessary for human self-realization and betterment, it is not sufficient to provide them all. A recent news item reports that 'Tokyo is jam-packed with 38 million people…but the city is one of the loneliest in the world. Almost a third of the population now lives by themselves and more and more are dying alone.' With traditional culture breaking down and no support systems to replace the contacts people formerly relied on, companies have sprung up to supply 'rental friends'.

Aside from those countries where internal strife is massively dislocating people, a 2013 Gallup migration survey shows that one-fifth to one-quarter of residents are on the move every five years within the US, New Zealand, Finland, and Norway, with 10 per cent or more of the population in several other nations following suit. People from diplomatic or military families are already quite familiar with this constant relocation.

On top of all this, it seems entirely possible—even probable—that the greater part of future generations (globally speaking) will not be able to own their own dwellings. While some can readily adapt to this new reality, for others, making a home in anonymous apartment buildings, housing blocks, condos, lofts, rooms, and various kinds of shared accommodation is a less rewarding prospect. Be this as it may, the fact is that in some parts of the world, such as Europe, people have long since adjusted to living in rented spaces, without suffering any apparent loss in quality of life or sense of home.

Given all the types of volatility and unpredictability that characterize the world today, one might wonder whether the concept of home has become attenuated and irrelevant. In a short essay entitled 'Were You Ever "At Home"?' Mel Thompson suggests that 'these days, the idea of having a "home" that somehow defines who we are has become problematic'. Factors he cites that mark major differences between the present and the past are people's general mobility, frequent travel, lives centred on work and the office, escapist activities, and boredom at home. Thompson asks, 'If there was one place you would really want to be able to return to over and over again, where would that be?' Some challenging issues are raised here, but perhaps this approach might itself be questioned. For, as argued in earlier chapters, we define our homes as much as they define us, and this is an ongoing, reciprocal process by which we construct our life's narrative. In addition, there need not be a single place that stands out as home to each of us. That situation may be a thing of the past; but even if it is, that does not negate the need and search for places of belonging, meaning, and mattering that play out in individual ways across the space and time of our lives. On the surface, home appears to have acquired a somewhat more casual and temporary quality for young people trying to make a go of it in the world, when they refer to their living quarters as 'my place' (North America) or 'at mine' (UK). But when questioned, most will call 'home' that special spot where they grew up; where they aspire to settle down; wherever they can be with those they love; where they can be themselves; or some combination of these.

Alternative living arrangements

Preserving and strengthening community are important preoccupations today and will no doubt continue to influence concepts of housing and the development of neighbourhoods into the future. 'Intentional communities' have gained popularity over the past few decades in the West. This designation refers to a pattern of dwelling whereby 'a group of people...have chosen to live with or near enough to each other to carry out their shared lifestyle or common purpose together. Families living in communities in the city, students living in student housing cooperatives near universities, and sustainability advocates living in rural back-to-the-land homesteads are all members of intentional communities.' This type of residential plan is already commonplace in many non-Western cultures. The idea of co-housing is that, while individuals or families can own their homes privately, they may also enjoy the use of common spaces such as playgrounds, community gardens, and a common house where meals are shared on a regular basis. Town houses are increasingly being built to embody at least some of these amenities. So-called 'retirement villages' are as well, although many seniors would prefer to live in interesting, mixed-generation neighbourhoods with or without co-housing set-ups.

Electronically enhanced homes

Some readers will already be experiencing the benefits of living in 'smart homes', that is, houses enhanced by automated technology that enables regulation of the operating and monitoring functions of various devices by smart phones or computers either within the domestic space or from elsewhere. One US-based website states that

> 'Smart Home' is the term commonly used to define a residence that
> has appliances, lighting, heating, air conditioning, TVs, computers,

entertainment audio & video systems, security, and camera systems that are capable of communicating with one another and can be controlled by a time schedule, from any room in the home, as well as remotely from any location in the world by phone or internet.

A UK-based website boasts that 'a smart home's refrigerator may be able to catalogue its contents, suggest menus, recommend healthy alternatives, and order replacements as food is used up. A smart home might even take care of feeding the cat and watering the plants.' These concepts give a whole new meaning to the declaration by modernist architect Le Corbusier that 'The house is a machine for living in'.

And what about robots? Didn't science fiction predict that they would take over all the essential functions of our homes? There are astonishing and remarkably rapid developments in the field of robotics, featuring machines with humanlike skills, behaviours, and appearances. But with the rise of the smart home, household robots may become redundant before they even gain entry. Their future role in the home might more likely become one of assisting elderly, infirm, handicapped, and lonely people to gain a better quality of life. It might remain to ask, though, how we could avoid calling a very sophisticated, autonomously operating smart home with centralized programming itself a kind of robot. Instead of preoccupying ourselves with concern over robot-dominated households, therefore, perhaps we should spend our precious worrying time on the implications of machines making workplaces obsolete and replacing substantial segments of the workforce. Perhaps we should meditate too on how people such as ourselves will fill more time, in the future—working or not—*at home*.

The Earth as home

For a very long time, indigenous peoples in many places have felt deep ties with the world around them, and have lived in respectful attunement with it. The cultures that came to be globally dominant, however, embraced an anthropocentric outlook—which many now believe to be flawed. This saw humans as utterly different from and independent of (or even hostile to) nature, and as beings that occupy the pinnacle of a presumed hierarchical order, the rest of which exists merely to serve our species' interests. After the world had been circumnavigated by sailing ships and increasingly accurate maps represented our planet as a globe, the totality of the Earth could be appreciated by people everywhere. The science of ecology (from the Greek word *oikos*: house, or more accurately inhabited house; domicile; dwelling; home), founded in the 19th century, and the first photos of Earth from outer space (see Figure 10), in the 20th, have revolutionized

10. NASA 'Blue Marble' photo of Earth from outer space (1972).

our ideas even further. The overall project of understanding our place in the scheme of things now seems to require a knowledge of our relationship to the natural world. And it seems at least possible that modern civilization might learn to view the Earth not merely as a storehouse of resources to be ruthlessly exploited, but as a home, a genuine dwelling place, a place of meaning, to be lovingly tended and protected as the miracle that it is. Thinking along these lines, perhaps radical action on climate change might even save some of the world's great cities and beautiful islands that people treasure as home.

Every end a new beginning

Our journey through the concept of home has taken us across the globe and out into the cosmos and back more than once. We have seen ourselves mirrored from many angles by what home means and stands for. We have explored the yearnings and aspirations that home signifies. These perspectives offer us the opportunity to enlarge our sense of self, and of what it means to belong in the world and to the human community. The insights gained from this adventure are tangible, as we learn how much we share in common, despite our differences, with people in other cultures, times, and places. The quest for home is ongoing and open-ended, as are the most interesting pursuits in life; and we will all continue to engage with it at our own pace and in our own ways.

References

Chapter 1: The many faces of home

'Façade': *Oxford Dictionary of English*, 2nd edn, ed. Catherine Soanes and Angus Stevenson (Oxford: Oxford University Press, 2003), p. 617.

Edwin Heathcote, *The Meaning of Home* (London: Frances Lincoln, 2012), p. 115.

'Home is where the heart is': often attributed to Roman philosopher Pliny the Elder.

Homer, *The Odyssey*, bk. 9.

Maya Angelou, *All God's Children Need Traveling Shoes* (New York: Vintage, 1991), p. 196.

Gaston Bachelard, *The Poetics of Space*, trans. Maria Jolas (Boston: Beacon Press, 1994).

Neutral, minimalist definition of home: <dictionary.reference.com/browse/home>.

OED expanded definition of 'home': 'home, n. 1 and adj.', OED Online. December 2014. Oxford University Press. <http://www.oed.com/view/Entry/87869?isAdvanced=false&result=1&rskey=krPUbt&>.

'Home on the Range': Daniel E. Kelley (music), John A. Lomax (1910 lyrics).

Alison Blunt and Robyn Dowling, *Home* (London: Routledge, 2006), p. 6.

'One of the dancers...': Peter Watson, *The Age of Nothing: How We Have Sought to Live Since the Death of God* (London: Weidenfeld & Nicolson, 2014), p. 46.

Edmunds Valdemārs Bunkše, *Geography and the Art of Life* (Baltimore: Johns Hopkins University Press, 2004), pp. 90, 93.

Anna Wierzbicka, *Imprisoned in English: The Hazards of English as a Default Language* (Oxford: Oxford University Press, 2014), p. xi.

Witold Rybczynski, *Home: A Short History of an Idea* (London: Heinemann, 1988), p. 62.

Jerry D. Moore, *The Prehistory of Home* (Berkeley: University of California Press, 2012), p. 7.

Meaning of *ngura*: Cliff Goddard, personal communication, 4 December 2014.

Polish word *dom*: Jerzy Bartmiński, *Aspects of Cognitive Ethnolinguistics*, ed. Jörg Zinken; trans. Adam Głaz (Sheffield: Equinox, 2009).

Hebrew word *bayit*: Philip Graubart, 'God Talk', *San Diego Jewish Journal*, September 2010; <http://sdjewishjournal.com/site/1146/god-talk-5>.

Nootka word for 'house': Michael Jackson, *At Home in the World* (Durham, NC: Duke University Press, 1995), p. 6.

Ludwig Wittgenstein, *Philosophical Investigations*, trans. G.E.M. Anscombe (Oxford: Basil Blackwell, 1953), secs. 66–71.

William Shakespeare, *Henry V*, 1.2.2; Samuel Taylor Coleridge, *Table Talk* (1821–34); Thornton Wilder, *The Matchmaker* (1954), in *Our Town, The Skin of Our Teeth, The Matchmaker* (Harmondsworth, Middlesex: Penguin, 1962), act 4, p. 267.

Clare Cooper Marcus, *House as a Mirror of Self: Exploring the Deeper Meaning of Home* (Berkeley, CA: Conari Press, 1995), p. 92.

Garrison Keillor, 'There's no place like home', *National Geographic*, 225/2 (February 2014), p. 67.

Michel de Montaigne, 'De l'institution des enfants' ('Of the Education of Children', 1579–80), from Michel de Montaigne, *Essais*; <http://www.livrefrance.com/Montaigne.pdf>; bk. 1, chap. 26, pp. 86, 87; trans. Michael Allen Fox.

Dan Kieran, *The Idle Traveller: The Art of Slow Travel* (Basingstoke, Hampshire: AA Publishing, 2013), p. 186.

Chapter 2: The importance of place

David Malouf, 'A spirit of play', in *A First Place* (Sydney: Vintage, 2015), p. 156.

'We live and move and have our being': Acts 17:28.

Alan Gussow, *A Sense of Place: The Artist and the American Land* (Washington, DC: Shearwater Books, 1997), p. 27.

Annie Dillard, *Pilgrim at Tinker Creek* (New York: Perennial Classics, 1998), p. 218.

Tiny houses: Ryan Mitchell, *Tiny House Living: Ideas for Building and Living Well in Less Than 400 Square Feet* (San Francisco: Betterway Home Books, 2012).

Julie Beck, 'The psychology of home: why where you live means so much', *The Atlantic*, 30 December 2011, p. 2; <http://www.theatlantic.com/health/archive/2011/12/the-psychology-of-home-why-where-you-live-means-so-much/249800>.

Otto F. Bollnow, 'Lived-space', trans. Dominic Gerlach, *Philosophy Today*, 5/1 (Spring 1961), pp. 32–3 (emphasis in original). (Text modified slightly in the interest of gender neutrality and greater inclusiveness.)

E. Relph, *Place and Placelessness* (London: Pion, 2008), Preface to reprint edn.

Martin Heidegger, 'Building dwelling thinking' (1954), in *Basic Writings*, rev. and exp. edn, ed. David Farrell Krell (San Francisco: HarperSanFrancisco, 1993), pp. 348–51 (emphasis in original).

Irene Watson, 'Spirituality', in Sarina Singh et al., *Aboriginal Australia & the Torres Strait Islands: Guide to Aboriginal Australia* (Melbourne: Lonely Planet, 2001), p. 110.

Anne Salmond, 'Theoretical landscapes: on a cross-cultural conception of knowledge', in David Parkin, ed., *Semantic Anthropology* (London: Academic Press, 1982), p. 85 (emphasis in original).

'Place and placelessness exist…': E. Relph, *Place and Placelessness* (London: Pion, 2008), Preface to reprint edition.

Barbara Bender, 'Place and landscape', in Christopher Tilley et al., eds, *Handbook of Material Culture* (London: Sage, 2006), p. 303.

Stan Rowe, *Home Place: Essays on Ecology*, rev. edn (Edmonton, Canada: NeWest Press, 2002), p. 31.

Jean-Jacques Rousseau, *Emile: Or Treatise on Education* (1762), trans. William H. Payne (Amherst, NY: Prometheus, 2003), p. 24.

Henry David Thoreau, 'Walking; or, the wild', *Atlantic Monthly*, June 1862, pt. 2, para. 24; <http://thoreau.eserver.org/walking2.html#wild>.

John Muir, *Our National Parks* (1901), p. 1; <http://vault.sierraclub.org/john_muir_exhibit/writings/our_national_parks/chapter_1.aspx>.

Bill Bryson, *At Home: A Short History of Private Life* (London: Black Swan, 2011), p. 504.

'Urban population growth', World Health Organization, Global Health Observatory (GHO) data; <http://www.who.int/gho/urban_health/situation_trends/urban_population_growth_text/en>.

India: 'Key facts and figures about India's population', *Open Knowledge*, 25 June 2014; <http://knowledge.allianz.com/demography/population/?1656/key-facts-and-figures-about-indias-population>.

E. Relph, *Place and Placelessness* (London: Pion, 2008), p. 40.

Chapter 3: Dwelling and dwellings

'Dwell': *Online Etymology Dictionary*; <http://www.etymonline.com/index.php?allowed_in_frame=0&search=dwell&searchmode=none>.

Mary Douglas, 'The idea of home: a kind of space', in Arien Mack, ed., *Home: A Place in the World* (New York: New York University Press, 1993), p. 263.

Jerry D. Moore, *The Prehistory of Home* (Berkeley: University of California Press, 2012), p. 3.

Evidence from South Africa: 'Archaeological discovery: earliest evidence of our cave-dwelling human ancestors', *ScienceDaily*, 21 December 2008; <http://www.sciencedaily.com/releases/2008/12/081219172137.htm>.

'Cliff dwellings', Mesa Verde National Park, National Park Service; <http://www.nps.gov/meve/learn/historyculture/cliff_dwellings_home.htm>.

Lloyd Kahn and Bob Easton, *Shelter* (Bolinas, CA: Shelter Publications, 1973), p. 5.

Kevin McCloud, 'The cave house', *Grand Designs*, UK Channel 4, 30 September 2015.

Katharine Greider, *The Archaeology of Home: An Epic Set on a Thousand Square Feet of the Lower East Side* (New York: Public Affairs, 2011), pp. 69–70.

'This is my home...': Joan Caravaggio, interviewed about Shoalhaven River flooding in New South Wales: 'Despite an expensive clean-up, she'll never sell', *ABC-TV 7:00 p.m. News* (Australia), 26 August 2015.

Paul Oliver, *Dwellings* (London: Phaidon Press, 2007), p. 216.

Benjamin Disraeli quoted in Bill Bryson, *At Home: A Short History of Private Life* (London: Black Swan, 2011), p. 301.

'Little boxes', composed by Malvina Reynolds; <http://people.wku. edu/charles.smith/MALVINA/mr094.htm>.

Dan Frank Kuehn, *Mongolian Cloud Houses: How to Make a Yurt and Live Comfortably* (Bolinas, CA: Shelter Publications, 2006), p. 2.

Buildings by Bruno Atkey and Jan Janzen: Lloyd Kahn, *Builders of the Pacific Coast* (Bolinas, CA: Shelter Publications, 2008), pp. 74–91, 136–7.

'Fallingwater', *Wikipedia*; <http://en.wikipedia.org/wiki/ Fallingwater>.

Buildings by Bill Heick and SunRay Kelley: Lloyd Kahn, *Builders of the Pacific Coast* (Bolinas, CA: Shelter Publications, 2008), pp. 220–1, 48–73.

Judith Flanders, *The Making of Home* (London: Atlantic Books, 2014), Introduction and p. 19.

Bill Bryson, *At Home: A Short History of Private Life* (London: Black Swan, 2011), pp. 55, 56.

Chapter 4: Remembering, imagining, and other mindwork

Marcel Proust, 'Combray', in *Remembrance of Things Past*, vol. 1: *Swann's Way*.

'Nostalgia': <http://www.thefreedictionary.com/nostalgia>.

Stephen Shaw, 'Returning home', *Phenomenology + Pedagogy* 8 (1990); <https://ejournals.library.ualberta.ca/index.php/pandp/article/ view/15140/11961>, p. 227.

Thomas Wolfe, *You Can't Go Home Again* (New York: Dell, 1960), pp. 70, 637 (emphasis in original).

Philip Glass, *Words Without Music: A Memoir* (New York: Liveright, 2015), p. 20.

Mai Al-Nakib, 'The hidden light of objects', in *The Hidden Light of Objects* (Doha: Bloomsbury Qatar Foundation, 2014), pp. 225, 232, 237 (emphasis in original).

Jessie Cole, 'Inner sanctum', *Sydney Morning Herald Good Weekend* magazine, 11 April 2015, p. 18.

'Beulah Land', composed by Mississippi John Hurt.

Brian Walsh, 'From housing to homemaking: worldviews and the shaping of home', *Christian Scholar's Review*, 35/2 (Winter 2006): <http://www.urbancentre.utoronto.ca/pdfs/housingconference/ Walsh_Housing_to_Homemaking.pdf>, p. 8.

Eman Abdelrahman Farah and Björn Klarqvist, 'Gender zones in the Arab Muslim house', *Proceedings of the 3rd International Space*

Syntax Symposium, Georgia Institute of Technology, Atlanta, GA, 7–11 May 2001, pp. 42.1, 42.2; <http://www.ucl.ac.uk/bartlett/3sss/papers_pdf/42_Farah&Klarquist.pdf>.

Tahiti; Pawnee First Nations earth lodges; 'Offerings were made…'; Burying the dead at home: Jerry D. Moore, *The Prehistory of Home* (Berkeley: University of California Press, 2012), pp. 173; 86, 88; 166; 95, 205, 206–7.

May/Midsummer rituals; Hunting rituals: James George Frazer, *The Golden Bough* (abridged edn) (New York: Dover, 2002), pp. 221f.; 120.

Cherokee 'townhouses': Jerry D. Moore, *The Prehistory of Home* (Berkeley: University of California Press, 2012), pp. 196–7.

Foundation-stone ritual: James George Frazer, *The Golden Bough* (abridged edn) (New York: Dover, 2002), p. 191.

Human body dreamed of as house: Sigmund Freud, *Introductory Lectures on Psycho-Analysis* (1915–16), pt. II, sec. X ('Symbolism in Dreams'), trans. James Strachey, in James Strachey, ed., *Standard Edition of the Complete Psychological Works of Sigmund Freud* (London: Hogarth Press and Institute of Psycho-Analysis, 1963), vol. XV, pp. 153, 159.

Dream-representation of self as house: C.G. Jung, *Symbols and the Interpretation of Dreams* (1961), in C.G. Jung, *The Symbolic Life: Miscellaneous Writings*, ed. Herbert Read et al., trans. R.F.C. Hall (London: Routledge & Kegan Paul, 1977), vol. 18, p. 213 (emphases in original); C.G. Jung, *The Tavistock Lectures* (1935), pt. II ('On the theory and practice of analytic psychology'), in *The Symbolic Life*, p. 42.

Houses symbolize the womb: Sigmund Freud, *Civilization and Its Discontents* (1930), The International Psycho-Analytical Library, ed. John D. Sutherland, No. 17; trans. Joan Riviere; rev. and newly ed. James Strachey (London: Hogarth Press and Institute of Psycho-Analysis, 1963), p. 28.

Chapter 5: People, objects, and identity

James Yandell, 'Foreword', to Clare Cooper Marcus, *House as a Mirror of Self: Exploring the Deeper Meaning of Home* (Berkeley, CA: Conari Press, 1995), pp. xiv, xv.

David Wästerfors, 'Fragments of home in youth care institutions', in Margarethe Kusenbach and Krista E. Paulsen, eds, *Home: International Perspectives on Culture, Identity, and Belonging* (Frankfurt am Main: Peter Lang, 2013), pp. 132, 130–1.

Polly Adler, *A House Is Not a* Home (1953), ed. Rachel Rubin (Amherst: University of Massachusetts Press, 2006).

Robert Ginsberg, 'Meditations on homelessness and being at home: in the form of a dialogue', in G. John M. Abbarno, ed., *The Ethics of Homelessness: Philosophical Perspectives* (Amsterdam: Rodopi, 1999), p. 31.

Robin Hobb, *Fool's Fate* (*Tawny Man Trilogy*, series 3) (New York: Bantam Spectra, 2004), p. 760.

Stephanie Perkins, *Anna and the French Kiss* (New York: Dutton, 2010), p. 250 (emphasis in original).

Sarah Dessen, *What Happened to Goodbye* (New York: Viking, 2011), pp. 364–5.

'The Minangkabau', *Anthropology and the Human Condition*, 8 November 2011; <http://sc2218.wikifoundry.com/page/The+Minangkabau>.

Kobena T. Hanson, 'Rethinking the Akan household: acknowledging the importance of culturally and linguistically meaningful images', *Africa Today*, 51 (2004), pp. 29, 30, 39.

Yi-Fu Tuan, *Space and Place: The Perspective of Experience* (Minneapolis: University of Minnesota Press, 1977), p. 18.

Karl Marx, *Capital* (1867), vol. 1, pt. 1, chap. 1, sec. 4.

Ian Woodward, *Understanding Material Culture* (Los Angeles: Sage, 2007), p. 158.

'Look' or 'style': see Anna Spiro, *Absolutely Beautiful Things: A Bright and Colourful Life* (Melbourne: Lantern Books, 2014).

James A. Tuedio, 'Thinking about home: an opening for discovery in philosophical practice'; <http://homelessness.philosophy.uoregon.edu/files/2014/02/Tuedio-1pwoi3p.pdf>, p. 2.

Self-actualization as universal: Louis Tay and Ed Diener, 'Needs and subjective well-being around the world', *Journal of Personality and Social Psychology*, 101 (2011): 354–65; <http://news.illinois.edu/news/11/0629happiness_EdDiener.html>.

Chapter 6: Home politics

Juliet A. Williams, 'The personal is political: thinking through the Clinton/Lewinsky/Starr Affair', American Political Science Association *PSOnline*, March 2001, p. 93; <http://journals.cambridge.org/download.php?file=%2FPSC%2FPSC34_01%2FS1049096501000142a.pdf&code=d4cd79ee8fba97f07005a5003ed21b36>.

Sarah A. Ellwood, 'Lesbian living spaces: multiple meanings of home', in Gill Valentine, ed., *From Nowhere to Everywhere: Lesbian Geographies* (New York: Routledge, 2011), p. 18.

Edwin Heathcote, *The Meaning of Home* (London: Frances Lincoln, 2012), p. 181.

Janet Zandy, 'Introduction', in Janet Zandy, ed., *Calling Home: Working-Class Women's Writings—An Anthology* (New Brunswick, NJ: Rutgers University Press, 1990), pp. 1–2, 5–6.

Interview with 'Kayla', in Shelley Mallett et al., *Moving Out, Moving On: Young People's Pathways In and Through Homelessness* (London: Routledge, 2010), p. 82.

Agnes Heller, 'Where are we at home?' *Thesis Eleven*, 41 (1995), p. 15.

Richard B. McKenzie, ed., *Home Away From Home: The Forgotten History of Orphanages* (New York: Encounter Books, 2009).

Nicholas Blomley, *Unsettling the City: Urban Land and the Politics of Property* (New York: Routledge, 2004), p. 110.

Hugh Brody, *The Other Side of Eden: Hunters, Farmers, and the Shaping of the World* (New York: North Point Press, 2001).

Ingetje Tadros, quoted in Dan Harrison, 'A long, slow road', *Sydney Morning Herald News Review*, 24–25 January 2015, pp. 32–3.

Xhosa people of South Africa: Diana Saverin, 'Long trek home for final resting place', *Guardian Weekly*, 24–30 July 2015, pp. 30–1; quotation from Rian Malan.

Robert Ginsberg, 'Meditations on homelessness and being at home: in the form of a dialogue', in G. John M. Abbarno, ed., *The Ethics of Homelessness: Philosophical Perspectives* (Amsterdam: Rodopi, 1999), p. 34.

Chapter 7: Homelessness and uprootedness

'Scholars have shown…': Nicholas Howe, ed., *Home and Homelessness in the Medieval and Renaissance World* (Notre Dame, IN: University of Notre Dame Press, 2004).

Tony Clark, cited by David Wilson, 'Hope bundled in a swag', *My Career, Sydney Morning Herald Business*, 4–5 July 2015, p. 15.

Mandy Nolan, *Home Truths: Myth Dusting by the Lady of the House* (Sydney: Finch Publishing, 2015), p. 49.

Patricia Anne Murphy, 'The rights of the homeless: an examination of the phenomenology of place', in G. John M. Abbarno, ed., *The*

Ethics of Homelessness: Philosophical Perspectives (Amsterdam: Rodopi, 1999), p. 60.

Suzanne Speak and Graham Tipple, 'Housing and homelessness in developing nations', in David Levinson, ed. *Encyclopedia of Homelessness* (Thousand Oaks, CA: Sage, 2004), vol. 1, p. 271.

Sophie Watson, with Helen Austerberry, *Housing and Homelessness: A Feminist Perspective* (London: Routledge & Kegan Paul, 1986), pp. 8–21, 167.

Gillian Triggs, 'Australian exceptionalism: human rights and executive power', Annual Sir Frank Kitto Lecture, University of New England, Armidale, NSW, Australia, 15 October 2014.

Syria: Khaled Hosseini, 'Syria's story of suffering too great to comprehend', *The Australian*, 22 July 2015, p. 10.

Emma Graham-Harrison, 'Kobani: destroyed and riddled with unexploded bombs, but its residents dare to dream of a new start', *The Guardian*, 1 February 2015; <http://www.theguardian.com/world/2015/jan/31/kobani-kurdish-forces-retake-isis-destroyed-power-sanitation-bombs-residents-hopes>.

Pakistan: '2011 Sindh floods', *Wikipedia*; <https://en.wikipedia.org/wiki/2011_Sindh_floods>.

Hurricane Katrina: Katy Reckdahl, 'The lost children of Katrina', *The Atlantic*, 2 April 2015; <http://www.theatlantic.com/education/archive/2015/04/the-lost-children-of-katrina/389345>.

Diego Garcia: Ari Shapiro, 'Islanders pushed out for U.S. base hope for end to 40-year exile', *Parallels*, US National Public Radio, 16 April 2015; <http://www.npr.org/sections/parallels/2015/04/16/399845336/hope-builds-for-islanders-displaced-in-shameful-chapter-of-u-k-history>.

'Diaspora'; 'transnational community': Khalid Koser, *International Migration: A Very Short Introduction* (Oxford: Oxford University Press, 2007), pp. 24–7.

Giselle Cohen, interviewed by Daisy Dumas, 'Diverse journeys', *Sydney Morning Herald*, News section, 24–25 January 2015, pp. 16–17.

Gurinder Chadha in *Who Do You Think You Are?* UK series 2, no. 6, BBC Two, 15 February 2006.

David Malouf, 'My multicultural life', in *A First Place* (Sydney: Vintage, 2015), pp. 30–1 (emphasis in original).

Noel Pearson, 'A rightful place: race, recognition and a more complete commonwealth', *Quarterly Essay*, 55 (September 2014), pp. 29–36.

'My biggest wish in life ...': Eqleema, quoted in *Making It Home: Real-Life Stories from Children Forced to Flee* (New York: Puffin Books, 2004), p. 31.

'We've made lots of new friends ...': Clarisse Kabwiz Tshiyena, quoted in *Making It Home: Real-Life Stories from Children Forced to Flee* (New York: Puffin Books, 2004), p. 52.

Daniel Miller, *Stuff* (Cambridge, UK: Polity, 2010), pp. 106–7.

Simone Weil, *The Need for Roots: Prelude to a Declaration of Duties Towards Mankind* (1949), trans. A.F. Wills (Milton Park, Abingdon, Oxon: London: Routledge Classics, 2002), p. 43.

Geörgy Lukács, *The Theory of the Novel: A Historico-Philosophical Essay on the Forms of Great Epic Literature* (1920), trans. Anna Bostock (Cambridge, MA: MIT Press), 1973, p. 34.

Peter L. Berger, Brigitte Berger, and Hansfried Kellner, *The Homeless Mind* (Harmondsworth, Middlesex: Penguin, 1974), pp. 62, 77, 166 (emphasis in original).

Susan Sontag, 'The anthropologist as hero' (1961), in *Against Interpretation and Other Essays* (New York: Picador USA, 1966), p. 69.

'Black people have been living in this culture for centuries ...': J.C. Faulk, interviewed by Sally Sara, '#BlackLivesMatter', *Foreign Correspondent*, ABC-TV (Australia), 7 December 2015.

Chapter 8: The future of home

Frederick A. Olafson, *Principles and Persons: An Ethical Interpretation of Existentialism* (Baltimore: Johns Hopkins University Press, 1967), p. 238.

Michael Jackson, *At Home in the World* (Durham, NC: Duke University Press, 1995), p. 123.

Abandoned villages of Europe: Simon Tisdall, 'Silent blight as the young leave villages for cities', *Guardian Weekly*, 28 August–3 September 2015, pp. 4–5.

'[S]ome of the oldest cities in the world ...': Aseem Inam, 'Chaos is an order we don't understand', Trulab: Laboratory for Designing Urban Transformation, 18 August 2014; <http://trulab.org/blog/2014/8/18/chaos-is-an-order-we-dont-understand>.

'A series of research studies ...': Madeleine Bunting, 'Rich Social Mix Makes Us More Tolerant', *Guardian Weekly* 190/15 (21–27 March 2014), p. 18.

K.O. Doyle, 'The symbolic meaning of house and home: an exploration in the psychology of goods', *American Behavioral Scientist* 35/6 (July/August 1992); <http://mymoney.pro/archives/1169>.

Atul Gawande, *Being Mortal: Illness, Medicine, and What Matters in the End* (London: Profile Books, 2014), pp. 76, 89 (emphasis in original).

Tokyo: 'Tokyo residents pay for friendship in lonely city', ABC-TV 7:00 p.m. News (Australia), 7 January 2015; <http://www.abc.net.au/news/2015-01-07/tokyo-residents-pay-for-friendship-in-lonely-city/6005480>.

Mel Thompson, 'Were you ever "at home"?', *The Philosopher's Beach Book* (London: Hodder Education, 2012), pp. 65–9.

'Intentional communities': Diana Leafe Christian, *Creating a Life Together: Practical Tools to Grow Ecovillages and Intentional Communities* (Gabriola Island, Canada: New Society Publications, 2003), p. xvi.

Smart homes: <http://www.smarthomeusa.com/smarthome>; <http://smarthomeenergy.co.uk/what-smart-home>.

Le Corbusier, 'Eyes which do not see: II. Airplanes' (1931), in *Towards a New Architecture*, trans. from the 13th French edn by Frederick Etchells (New York: Dover, 1986), p. 4.

Further reading

Chapter 1: The many faces of home

Benjamin, David N. et al., eds, *The Home: Words, Interpretations, Meanings and Environments* (Aldershot: Avebury, 1995).

Gordon, Mary, *Home: What It Means and Why It Matters* (New York: Sterling, 2010).

Mack, Arien, ed., *Home: A Place in the World* (New York: New York University Press, 1993).

Pearlman, Mickey, ed., *A Place Called Home: Twenty Writing Women Remember* (New York: St. Martin's Press, 1996).

Perlman, Jim et al., eds, *The Heart of All That Is: Reflections on Home* (Duluth, MN: Holy Cow! Press, 2013).

Chapter 2: The importance of place

Allen, John S., *Home: How Habitat Made Us Human* (New York: Basic Books, 2015).

Casey, Edward S., *Getting Back into Place: Toward a Renewed Understanding of the Place-World*, 2nd edn (Bloomington: Indiana University Press, 2009).

Feld, Steven and Keith H. Basso, eds, *Senses of Place* (Sante Fe: School of American Research Press, 1996).

Read, Peter, *Belonging: Australians, Place and Aboriginal Ownership* (Cambridge, UK: Cambridge University Press, 2000).

Sanders, Scott Russell, *Staying Put: Making Home in a Restless World* (Boston: Beacon Press, 1993).

Chapter 3: Dwelling and dwellings

Campo, Juan Eduardo, *The Other Sides of Paradise: Explorations into the Religious Meanings of Domestic Space in Islam* (Columbia: University of South Carolina Press, 1991).

Kamo no Chōmei, 'The ten foot square hut' (1212), *Mountain Road: The Zen Practitioner's Journal* 21/2 (Winter 2002); <http://www.mro.org/mr/archive/21-2/articles/tenfoothut.html>. Also available in *Four Huts: Asian Writings on the Simple Life*, trans. Bruce Watson (Boston: Shambhala, 1994), pp. 39–84.

Marshall, Joseph M. III, *To You We Shall Return: Lessons about Our Planet from the Lakota* (New York: Sterling Ethos, 2010).

Pryor, Francis, *Home: A Time Traveller's Tales From British Prehistory* (London: Allen Lane, 2014).

Seamon, David and Robert Mugerauer, *Dwelling, Place and Environment: Towards a Phenomenology of Person and World* (Dordrecht: Martinus Nijhoff, 1985).

Chapter 4: Remembering, imagining, and other mindwork

Burger, Jerry M., *Returning Home: Reconnecting with Our Childhoods* (Lanham, MD: Rowman & Littlefield, 2011).

Kavanagh, Jennifer, *Journey Home: An Exploration of Our Inner and Outer Identity* (Alresford, Hants: John Hunt, 2012).

Kron, Joan, *Home-Psych: The Social Psychology of Home and Decoration* (New York: Clarkson N. Potter, 1983).

Wakely, Mark, *Dream Home* (Crows Nest, NSW: Allen & Unwin, 2003).

Wilson, Janelle L., *Nostalgia: Sanctuary of Meaning* (Lewisburg, PA: Bucknell University Press, 2005).

Chapter 5: People, objects, and identity

Akhtar, Salman, *Objects of Our Desire: Exploring Our Intimate Connections with the Things Around Us* (New York: Harmony Books, 2005).

Aries, Philippe and Georges Duby, gen. eds, *A History of Private Life*, 5 vols. Trans. Arthur Goldhammer (Cambridge, MA: Belknap Press of Harvard University Press, 1992–8).

Attfield, Judy, *Wild Things: The Material Culture of Everyday Life* (Oxford: Berg, 2000).

Jarrett, Grant, ed., *The House That Made Me: Writers Reflect on the Places and People That Defined Them* (Tempe, AZ: SparkPress, 2016).

Menzel, Peter, *Material World: A Global Family Portrait* (San Francisco: Sierra Club Books, 1994).

Chapter 6: Home politics

Briganti, Chiara and Kathy Mezei, eds, *The Domestic Space Reader* (Toronto: University of Toronto Press, 2012).

Chapman, Tony, *Gender and Domestic Life: Changing Practices in Families and Households* (Basingstoke: Palgrave Macmillan, 2004).

Hardy, Sheila, *A 1950s Housewife: Marriage and Homemaking in the 1950s* (Stroud, Gloucestershire: The History Press, 2011).

Hayden, Dolores, *Redesigning the American Dream: The Future of Housing, Work and Family Life* (New York: W.W. Norton, 2002).

Johnson, Lesley and Justine Lloyd, *Sentenced to Everyday Life: Feminism and the Housewife* (Oxford: Berg, 2004).

Chapter 7: Homelessness and uprootedness

Ahmed, Sara et al., eds, *Uprootings/Regroundings: Questions of Home and Migration* (Oxford: Berg, 2003).

Al-Ali, Nadje and Khalid Koser, eds, *New Approaches to Migration? Transnational Communities and the Transformation of Home* (London: Routledge, 2002).

Al-Sabouni, Marwa, *The Battle for Home: The Vision of a Young Architect in Syria* (London: Thames & Hudson, 2016).

Eidse, Faith and Nina Sichel, eds, *Uprooted Childhoods: Memoirs of Growing Up Global* (London: Nicholas Brealey; Boston: Intercultural Press, 2004).

Porteous, J. Douglas and Sandra E. Smith, *Domicide: The Global Destruction of Home* (Montréal: McGill-Queen's University Press, 2001).

Tapscott, Mike, *Homeless Hero: Understanding the Soul of Home* (Bloomington, IN: Abbott Press, 2013).

Chapter 8: The future of home

Chapin, Ross, *Pocket Neighborhoods: Creating Small-Scale Community in a Large-Scale World* (Newtown, CT: Taunton Press, 2011).

Geffen, Susan B., *Take That Nursing Home and Shove It! How to Secure an Independent Future for Yourself and Your Loved Ones* (Redondo Beach, CA: Sage Press, 2013).

Legge, Kylie, *Future City Solutions* (Sydney: Place Partners, 2013).

McCamant, Kathryn and Charles Durrett, *Creating Cohousing: Building Sustainable Communities* (Gabriola Island, BC: New Society Publishers, 2011).

Peterson, M. Nils, Tarla Rai Peterson, and Jianguo Liu, *The Housing Bomb: Why Our Addiction to Houses Is Destroying the Environment and Threatening Our Society* (Baltimore: Johns Hopkins University Press, 2013).

Publisher's acknowledgements

We are grateful for permission to include the following copyright material in this book.

Extract taken from O.F. Bollnow, 'Lived-Space', *Philosophy Today*, Volume 5, Issue 1, Spring 1961, pp. 31–2, DOI: 10.5840/philtoday1961513.

Lyrics from the song 'Beulah Land', composed by Mississippi John Hurt, copyright Mississippi John Hurt music, administered by Adage songs.

Lyrics from the song 'Little Boxes', words and music by Malvina Reynolds © Schroder Music Co. (ASCAP) 1962, Renewed 1990. Used by permission, all rights reserved.

Extract taken from Simone Weil, *The Need for Roots: Prelude to a Declaration of Duties Towards Mankind* (London: Routledge Classics, 2002), p. 43.

The publisher and author have made every effort to trace and contact all copyright holders before publication. If notified, the publisher will be pleased to rectify any errors or omissions at the earliest opportunity.

Index

Home

Index

SOCIAL MEDIA
Very Short Introduction

Join our community

www.oup.com/vsi

- Join us online at the official Very Short Introductions
  Facebook page.
- Access the thoughts and musings of our authors with our
  online **blog**.
- Sign up for our monthly **e-newsletter** to receive information
  on all new titles publishing that month.
- Browse the full range of Very Short Introductions online.
- Read **extracts** from the Introductions for free.
- If you are a teacher or lecturer you can order inspection
  copies quickly and simply via our website.